Partnership in the Gospel

Partnership in the Gospel

Seven Exercises in Liberal Biblical Theology

Robert Allan Hill

RESOURCE *Publications* • Eugene, Oregon

PARTNERSHIP IN THE GOSPEL
Seven Exercises in Liberal Biblical Theology

Copyright © 2024 Robert Allan Hill. All rights reserved. Except for brief quotations in critical publications or reviews, no part of this book may be reproduced in any manner without prior written permission from the publisher. Write: Permissions, Wipf and Stock Publishers, 199 W. 8th Ave., Suite 3, Eugene, OR 97401.

Resource Publications
An Imprint of Wipf and Stock Publishers
199 W. 8th Ave., Suite 3
Eugene, OR 97401

www.wipfandstock.com

PAPERBACK ISBN: 978-1-6667-8204-2
HARDCOVER ISBN: 978-1-6667-8205-9
EBOOK ISBN: 978-1-6667-8206-6

VERSION NUMBER 03/21/24

Portions of this book appeared previously in *Charles River: Essays and Meditations for Daily Reading* by Robert Allan Hill. United States: Resource Publications, 2015.

Scripture quotations unless otherwise noted are from the New Revised Standard Version Bible, copyright © 1989 by the Division of Christian Education of the National Council of the Churches of Christ in the U.S.A., and are used by permission. All rights reserved.

Scripture quotations marked KJV are from The Authorized (King James) Version. Rights in the Authorized Version in the United Kingdom are vested in the Crown. Reproduced by permission of the Crown's patentee, Cambridge University Press.

Quotation marked *Book of Discipline* is from *The Book of Discipline of The United Methodist Church—2008*. Copyright © 2008 by The United Methodist Publishing House. Used by Permission.

Contents

Acknowledgments | vii
Introduction | ix

1 An Initial Exercise in Liberal Biblical Theology | 1
2 "No Male and Female": Ruminations on the New Creation | 23
3 Mark | 51
4 Luke | 65
5 Matthew | 76
6 John | 91
7 The Difference Easter Makes | 110
8 Afterward | 132

Bibliography | 135

Acknowledgments

WE BEGIN WITH A word of gratitude to the esteemed and excellent professors who have provided academic formation and guidance regarding the Bible, and its interpretation, over the course of many years and decades.

Lloyd Easton, a fifth generation Boston Personalist, and his philosophy department at Ohio Wesleyan University gave a rigorous immersion in philosophy both ancient and modern, from Plato to the existentialists, with frequent, if critical, reflection on the Holy Scripture.

I am grateful for my teachers at the Union Theological Seminary in the City of New York, who together sparked and sustained a lifetime of love of the Bible, love of the strange world of the Bible. Raymond Brown and J. Louis Martyn in biblical studies; Cyril Richardson in patristics (then so called); Christopher Morse and James Cone in philosophical theology; and James Forbes and William Sloane Coffin in homiletics (classroom and pulpit). These provided as fine a grounding in the history of theology as one could desire. Martyn, in particular, has had a lastingly personal impact on my life work in preaching and teaching.

At McGill University, the sharp and complementary perspectives on the Hebrew Scriptures and the New Testament drew us on into further depth and breadth in understanding. My freedom to study with the esteemed Dr. Frederik Wisse and Rev. Dr. N. T.

ACKNOWLEDGMENTS

Wright was a precious gift. A Methodist bishop willing to appoint us to two churches in the north woods, a young family willing to live and work there, an aunt who gave us an old car to drive, and a Canadian University of the first water willing to receive an unproven immigrant made this freedom possible.

A great cloud of witnesses round about all these, clergy in large measure from the Methodist tradition, aided and expanded the gifts given in Ohio and New York and Montreal. Thank you, one and all.

Introduction

THE APOSTLE TO THE gentiles approached his beloved Philippians with a choice phrase, *koinonia tou euaggeliou*,[1] the partnership in the gospel, the partnership of the gospel, the sharing in the gospel, the fellowship of the gospel, the commonwealth of the gospel. Rev. Ken McMillan, our dear friend now of blessed memory, quietly and memorably and steadily used this phrase in the course of his gentle pastoral ministry as the longtime senior pastor in the United Methodist Church in Long Beach, California.[2] Every autumn, when the senior ministers of the large UMC churches gathered for mutual support and edification, his was neither the loudest voice, nor the most pronounced, nor the most frequently lifted. For all that, his example and inclination in faith continue to resound, in some ways far more fully than others, and especially as an incarnation of Philippians 1:5.

The method by which Ken came to the full and vital pastoral expression of faith, and to his own rendering of the Scripture in preaching the gospel, is at the heart of this book—not in a personal sense, but in an exemplary one. With assurance and grace, Ken could scour the Scriptures, locate the gospel, and move

1. Phil 1:5. Author's preferred translation is "partnership in the gospel."
2. See Ken's obituary for an introduction to his liberal outlook, his liberal leaning, his liberal biblical theology. Archbold, "Pastor fought for equal rights," October 30, 2018.

INTRODUCTION

along forward in partnership with others. So shall we proceed here. This book offers exercises—angles of perspective—with regard to biblical theology, which may support others, clergy and lay, along the path of faith.

The heyday of biblical theology is long past, and the use of the phrase far less frequent, in church or in school, than once it was. The very use of the singular in the phrase raises hackles for some, and not without reason. Of course, in Holy Scripture there are multiples of theologies, and many faith traditions. Today, most of theological education in biblical studies emphasizes the diversities and varieties of these, past and present. Students learn, to some extent, the wide sweep of biblical authority considered among these, even the integral distinction of what it means to be a *sola scriptura* tradition, of affirming the Scripture as the sole source of religious authority. My own denomination, Methodism, is not a *sola scriptura* tradition—we are not Baptists, Calvinists, or Lutherans. Methodism respects Scripture as primary, not exclusive, and the foundation for diverse interpretation. Our discussion in these pages takes place with the understanding that the Bible is primary, foundational, fundamental, basic, prototypical—but not exclusively authoritative.

But any preacher entering the pulpit on a seven-day basis, and any lay leader or teacher of a gathered group of people set to reading a particular book in Hebrew Scripture or in the New Testament, must have some abiding sense of not only the varieties of biblical theology—and, hence, the "varieties of religious experience,"[3] as one other Bostonian once put it—but must also have some overarching grasp of what the Bible, as a whole, is about. It is this understanding of the Bible's unifying themes, grounded in a solid knowledge of biblical study, that this book attempts to exercise, toward a liberal biblical theology.

What we mean by liberal, here—to preempt the question— is to say: not traditional, conservative, fundamental, orthodox; but also, not progressivist, successivist, anarchist, liberationist, or Marxist. Liberal as Tillich was to theology, as Berlin was to

3. James, *Varieties of Religious Experience*.

INTRODUCTION

political science, as Tittle was to homiletics, as Thurman was to culture, and so on. Not rigid, not bound, but rather experiencing the true freedom of new creation in Christ, the offer and promise of which sings from the Bible's sixty-six books. It is no accident that the word "liberal" shares its root with "liberty," freedom by another name. We will return often, in these pages, to the biblical theme of freedom, our experience of freedom in Christ, a theme at the core of our discussion.

Liberal biblical Methodist theology thus considers Scripture (the Bible as an authority), experience (we have been liberated through Christ), tradition (our beloved UMC), and reason (mind). Scripture sits alongside experience and tradition and reason. One Harvard graduate, a dear clergy friend, at a lakeside luncheon once responded with animus to a reference to Scripture: "Ah, there we go, the Bible rearing its ugly head again." There is surely ugliness in the Bible. But beauty there is, as well. The undergirding unities, the structures of height and thought that give parts the support of the whole, remind us so.

Our discussion owes its shape to John Wesley and to the Anglican theological tradition upon which he stood. Wesley emphasized the unity of Scripture, experience, tradition, and reason—four modalities, four "sides" of Wesley's theological quadrilateral, which each illuminate one angle of a mature Christian faith. Experience weaves into our shared history and enlightens us when we choose to examine it. Tradition stands upon the growth and development of faith, over centuries past and across diverse cultures. And reason—those processes of continual discovery, discernment, and rational thought—forms the basis for the application of faith in our lives. Each side is a means by which to view the others. While we might barely see by the light of one candle, we see clearly by the light of four.

Many of our current lasting controversies in American Christianity are due, in part, to the willingness of conservatives to champion scripture and tradition while leaving reason and experience to the liberals, and to the willingness of liberals to champion reason and experience while leaving scripture and tradition to conservatives. The liberal biblical theological voice, once quite strong, say, sixty years ago, has fallen silent. It is a somewhat superannuated outlook today, but for that reason it is more needed, rather than less. One longs for those who will strive to maintain the liberal balance.

Put another way, a comparison with legal theories might help. There is a parallel to be drawn between legal originalism and biblical literalism. We are right now under the sad sway of those who champion, in legal theory, the perspective of originalism. "Originalism contends that the Constitution should be interpreted and enforced on the basis of its 'original meaning,' namely what it meant when it was adopted,"[4] explained writer David Cole, who in nearly the same breath opined that "the simplicity and objectivity that originalism promises are a charade."

The response offered to legal originalism is "common law constitutional interpretation,"[5] which "starts with the text of the Constitution but recognizes that the ways its broad and open-ended provisions apply will be elucidated gradually over time as judges confront particular cases and seek to make sense of what has gone before, analogize from precedent to contemporary circumstances, and explain their reasoning to provide guidance for the future."[6] *Text, experience, tradition, and reason:* Wesley's quadrilateral, seen from a different light.

Legal originalism is to constitutionalism as biblical literalism is to liberalism. Biblical literalism needs and deserves a response—a clear and concise response—to its own abiding senses of unity, its own claims to authority, from a perspective that is fully liberal yet equally invested in the truth, beauty, and goodness of Scripture. A compelling response to biblical literalism will return tradition, experience, and reason to their rightful places within our fullest understanding of faith. We will look to

---

4. Cole, "Originalism's Charade," 18–20. See also, by Boston University law professor James E. Fleming, *Constructing Basic Liberties: A Defense of Substantive Due Process*. Chicago: University of Chicago Press, 2022.

5. Strauss, "Common Law Constitutional Interpretation," 63 (3): 877.

6. Cole, "Originalism's Charade."

INTRODUCTION

tradition to remember the heart of the gospel message as it was meant. We will look to experience—of freedom, of new creation in Christ, of Presence—to appropriate the faith for ourselves. And we will look to reason to judge and apply those principles of faith which shape the experience of so many others.

The United Methodist Church has before it the task of interpreting the *missio Dei*, the mission of God, and our response to it in worship and in service as it will apply to the work of the church. How do we think about faith, together, and in light of our experiences, sacred texts, and church traditions? How do we compare traditional models of morality with new creational models? How do we, reasonably, disagree with each other? What is the basis of unity, and how do we preserve such unity as we move forward in this modern age?

It may be that only after some years of dogged and difficult work in preaching and teaching, in interpretation, one draws up, pauses, and becomes ready for these kinds of exercises. The audience for these chapters might include laypeople, volunteers guiding others in reading the Gospels; or teachers, professors well-versed in biblical studies but wanting a closer familiarity with the unifying themes of the Scriptures; or denominational leaders searching for ways to guide one of the churches of the Church forward through what is surely a time of fracture, of social dislocation.

But these groups, even when sown together, are not the main audience for this work in liberal biblical theology. The audience for this book centrally includes a minister—four or fourteen or twenty-four years graduated from a school of theology—who realizes, however dimly, the need to return to a more rigorous consideration of biblical theological perspective, in order to provide the strong, stable grounding one needs in preaching, in pastoral care, in congregational leadership, and in social witness.

Such is a lifetime of work, and such is a matter of labor, homework, diligence, and prayerful attention, morning by morning, in the minister's study or the layperson's den. Hence, this book involves a series of chapters devoted to particular forms of exercise—call them spiritual workouts—meant to enhance an appreciation for a

INTRODUCTION

liberal biblical theology. In certain places, we incorporate experience, tradition, and reason as means by which to interpret Scripture. In others, we interpret Scripture as the means by which to integrate the context of our own life and ministry. Chapter by chapter, these pages offer forms of engagement in exercise.

In what we might consider a primer, a survey course in liberal biblical theology, Chapter 1 faces, head-on, the question of commonality within diversity, of the need for a primordial overlook regarding what holds those sixty-six sacred books together, of what makes the Bible—well, the Bible. Here we study the older insights of G.B. Caird comparatively with the author's current work in this area, and we discuss three unifying themes found across the whole of the Scriptures: presence, freedom, and experience.

Chapter 2 presents, *exemplum docet*, a systemic argument toward the just, participatory, and sustainable resolution of the current dilemma for the United Methodist Church in our time: the heated debate regarding the full humanity of gay people. This chapter attempts to bring reason and a liberal biblical theology grounded in Galatians to this fraught theological conflict and biblical conundrum.

Chapters 3, 4, and 5 climb up and down the hillsides of the Synoptic Gospels. The hope is that these chapters—together, through comparative observance of their shared yet distinctive overtures to liberal biblical theology, and separately, through useful and perhaps new methodologies which one might employ during the course of independent interpretation of Scripture—might exercise our ways of thinking critically, about the Gospels or about any biblical passage. Mark (Chapter 3) unfolds from the ground up: building from the materials of theology, biblical context, and careful deliberation a sound conceptual scaffolding on which to stand. Luke (4) unfolds from the past forward, revealing the insight to be gained from a comparative approach that appreciates earlier sources of interpretation. And Matthew (5) unfolds along the permeable border between history and religion—which is to say, between narrative and doctrine—in an

INTRODUCTION

attempt to exercise our reason and judgement through distinction within a vast field of study.

Chapter 6 surveys, at some length, the Gospel of John: the windswept, craggy, icy high peak of Holy Scripture that is the Fourth Gospel. We review John's distinctive liberal biblical theology, so different from those found in the Synoptic Gospels—the difference of an "embraceable variant."[7] The Fourth Gospel affirms our life experiences of disappointment, of dislocation, and of departure, and returns to us freedom, grace, and love. And, with those three, it presents an invitation to variance in our own time.

At the close, Chapter 7 looks at Easter—the central Christian affirmation, and hence a profoundly unifying one—through pastoral and sermonic lenses, with the invitation to ongoing homiletical work. Easter, by its wonderous nature, evokes a liberal biblical theology, and its annual celebration is an opportunity to deepen our faith and our connection to a liberal biblical theology. Some preparation, some practice in thought, is necessary to speak to the abiding vistas, the highest hopes, the unifying themes of the Scriptures.

To those interested in further exploration, an afterward offers directions toward five other forms of exercise. It should be added that there is no postlude here, no conclusion following the seven exercises, in the hope that those who exercise in this gymnasium will go forth and, in so doing, will add their chapters to what is surely, by its very nature, a most unfinished symphony of exercises in liberal biblical theology.

---

7. Brown, *Community of the Beloved Disciple*, 91.

1

An Initial Exercise in Liberal Biblical Theology

WE BEGIN, ALWAYS, IN gratitude: for the esteemed and excellent professors who have provided academic formation and guidance regarding the Bible, and its interpretation, over the course of many years and decades; and for the great cloud of witnesses, clergy in large measure from the Methodist tradition, round about all these, who aided and expanded the gift of understanding. Their varied influence—coming, as they did, from many different backgrounds and perspectives—provided a foundation with which to perceive commonality within diversity. Among their teachings, and amid their humanity, and by way of our apperception of God's grace, emerge common themes that allow for the reconciliation of difference.

One example, hopefully a clear and compelling one, of what these blessed mentors and teachers did provide is offered in this chapter's reflection on the main theme of the book. The suggestion within this exercise is that each one of us, as interpreters of Scripture, will to some manner and degree need to move through its marvelous diversity to its mystic, mysterious unity. One who has the privilege and responsibility to scour the Scriptures in search of a sermon every seven days also lives with an ongoing need to hone one's considered understanding of the Bible as not only a collection of varied and diverse gems and treasures, but also an authoritative collection that carries an abiding unity, if not always a strict unanimity.

It falls to us, then, to recognize commonality within the diversity of the Bible in the same manner that we recognize the common grace within our shared humanity. We may, as you will read below, find grace during a roadside encounter with a lost trucker in frigid darkness. We may find it in the words of a poem that brings us closer to its author, or closer to God. We may find it in chances given us, over the course of a life, to freely learn and live. To recognize such experience, such presence, such freedom—some common threads of God's grace—is to recognize some common threads within the diversity of our earthly existence, and to grow our connection to the divine.

This essay, written for the McGill University community, was delivered in October of 2022 at McGill and more broadly by electronic means across Quebec and Canada as the University Lecture for the School of Religious Studies. It was first published in *Journal of the Council for Research on Religion* and appears here as originally offered.

An Exercise in Liberal Biblical Theology: McGill University Lecture and Symposium, October 21, 2022[1]

I. Frontispiece

My intention, for these fifty minutes and six thousand words, is to engage us in an exercise in liberal biblical theology, which may serve into the future as an example for such conversation among

---

1. Originally published in a slightly different form in *Journal of the Council for Research on Religion* 4, no. 2 (August 2023): 81–94. Reprinted by permission of the author and the publisher.

neighbors within and alongside the global church, as we ponder theological education for the twenty-first century. The exercise also intentionally carries some personal memoir conjured in connection with a return, after many years, to these hallowed halls, laden as they are with both clear and murky chords of memory.

Jan and I are honored and pleased to be included in your fine symposium this autumn. It is a homecoming of sorts for us, returning to life along University Street in Montreal, after the better part of forty years. We extend our thanks and sincere gratitude to all who have made the trip possible. Ms. Amanda Rosini, a PhD candidate, a co-editor of *Arc: The Journal of the School of Religious Studies* (which journal has given many of us a route toward early publication), has epitomized hospitality. Professor Dr. Patricia Kirkpatrick, a colleague and friend over the four decades since her memorable arrival at McGill in the mid-1980s, brought the warmth of invitation in the cold of Covid, and kept the trip alive in the imagination over many months and over against the prevailing winds of Covid protocols. Professor Director Dr. Garth Green, a friend since 2006 and former colleague at Boston University, and his wonderful family, have a glad place in our happy memories of earlier work done in "the home of the bean and the cod."[2] Garth was a sometime teacher of our son Benjamin, before Ben shifted from pastoral to legal education (not to say, from grace to law). Of reading law and reading theology, Ben said: *the legal material is pretty straightforward, but they are very harsh in the teaching of it; theology is completely inscrutable, but they are very kind in the teaching of it.* In his own reading of theology, Garth keeps alive that balance between the straightforward and the inscrutable.

Two groups, also, at the last need mention: one, those present in actual or virtual space today, who have given of your time that we might learn together; the other, McGill University, which allowed to grant me a PhD in 1991 after a decade of travel and study, and which

2. *New York Times*, "An Immortal Poem," July 6, 1923. This reference to Boston comes from a quatrain credited to John C. Bossidy based on his recitation during an alumni dinner at Holy Cross College: "And this is good old Boston, / The home of the bean and the cod, / Where the Lowells talk to the Cabots, / And the Cabots talk only to God."

has now given the further honor of this morning, this remembrance of things past, and this moment. Thank you, one and all.

Speaking of travel and study: for some years, I drove several times a week across the border from northern New York to Canada ("down into Canada" as we put it, speaking in topographical and not geographical terms). Every day the same questions were posed at the border: What is your name? Where are you from? Where are you headed? Do you have anything to declare? These are existential questions of identity, history, mystery, and adaptability. These same questions meet us when we cross the border into what James Smart called "the strange silence of the Bible in the church."[3]

John Wesley wanted to become *homo unius libri*,[4] which is to say: a person of one book, the Bible. But in our time, it might be said that while we have known bits and parts—parables and commandments, say—of the Holy Scripture, we may not have had enough chance or encouragement to ask big, broad questions of the Bible. On those questions, in the end, depends any interpretation of the Bible's various parts, and on those questions, in the end, any community—in the sense of love of neighbor—also depends.

What holds the Bible together, if anything? How did this remarkably diverse collection emerge into a rough-and-ready unity? How do we think about the Divine Presence, the elusive presence expressed in the Holy Scripture and found there by centuries of readers well before us? What does such presence mean to us? How do we adapt its wonders to the actual daily experience of life in community, of struggle in faith, of prayer and song?

Identity. History. Mystery. Adaptability. We, or I, may not have done, over the last two generations, what we could and should have done with some of the big questions, some of the primary questions concerning the Bible and its view of life, its theology, even its liberal biblical theology. Or, to put it another way: what we *have* done has perhaps been limited, by means of language and conversation, mostly to those who live at a bit of distance from life and church, from challenge and choice (that is a kind way of

---

3. Smart, *Strange Silence of the Bible*.
4. Wesley, *Wesley's Standard Sermons*, 32.

speaking of myself, and other academics along the way). In this morning hour, with a little help from some friends, and with more than a little help from the prayers, good questions, and responses from a responsive audience (you all, and all you all), we will try to engage in a lively and accessible exercise in liberal biblical theology. Our desired outcome is this: that the heart of the Bible might become more familiar, more accessible, more graspable, and so, we trust, more *helpful* to us in our walk of faith, day by day, and in our love of neighbor, day by day. For we each, as did Mr. Wesley, harbor a desire to become *homo unius libri*.

The drives "down into Canada" I mentioned a moment ago were a consequence of traveling many days each week between our small country parsonage in New York State and McGill University in Montreal, where I studied Coptic texts for my doctoral work in New Testament studies. I never completely lost my sense of anticipation, even dread, at the existential questions posed to me at the border; nor did I lose my awareness of the weather, which practiced its own form of existential questioning. I twice put the car into snowbanks, once on each side of the border. As I crossed the Saint Lawrence into Montreal by way of the Mercier bridge, I would see bumper stickers that read, if memory serves: *Priez pour moi, je conduis sur le pont Mercier.*

One very cold morning, near five a.m., while driving in the dark down beyond Huntingdon, Quebec, I stopped in the snow alongside a lost trucker. I lowered the window to catch his question: "*Où est la frontière?*" After I had finally translated to myself his simple query, "Where is the border," I leaned back and haltingly replied in French; but before I could say much, he caught my accent (or maybe it was my abysmal grammar). Jumping for joy, he said, "Buddy, you speak English! You must be American." And I could say to him, in the language that we shared, "You are not far, not far at all from the border."

We feel a surprising, joyful anticipation as we approach the border in faith. In some ways, every soulful reading of Scripture, whether public or private, is such an approach. In use at the border is the same language we have used for a lifetime: the language of grace.

We cross the same border with every confession of sin and every acceptance of pardon. We cross the same border with every awareness of idolatry and every word of forgiveness. We have crossed over before in the daylight, so that when night falls, we need not fear. We know what the Psalmist meant by the words, "Weeping may linger for the night, but joy comes with the morning."[5]

II. An Essay by G.B. Caird

Each time I crossed the border, upon reaching McGill University, I found myself with a precious gift: the freedom to study. I studied especially the Coptic Gnostic documents from Nag Hammadi, under the guidance of one of their translators and most knowledgeable interpreters, the esteemed Dr. Frederik Wisse. I studied under, and served as teaching assistant to, a relatively unknown Anglican priest who has since become a best-selling Christian author, Rev. Dr. N. T. Wright.

One winter day, I found myself on the wrong floor of the library, not the one I should have been on. Time travel with me for a moment. This was in the 1980s, which is to say that a student still spent a fair amount of time not in looking at a computer screen, but in hunting down books among the musty and dusty stacks of a well filled library. You might, after getting disoriented in the lower depths of the cavernous library searching for one specific item, find yourself in curiosity browsing through things you had no plan to look at. These days, we have far less need to spend time walking up and down aisles in dilapidated bookstores or crowded libraries, where and when something unexpected might surprise us; but once upon a time, the antique practice of hunting in the library stacks could, sometimes, produce a marvel.

On this winter day, I found myself browsing through collections of speeches that had been given at McGill. Why? I have no idea. But in that pause and perusal, of a sudden, I came upon a collection of inaugural lectures from past decades at McGill,

---

5. Ps 30:5, NRSV.

including one lecture by G. B. Caird that I subsequently photocopied. Its title: "The New Testament View of Life."

In 1951, Caird courageously set out to do a portion of what we are trying to do this morning: to consider some comprehensive questions about the Bible, to gain a foothold, to make an overture to biblical theology. With courage he assayed to raise and answer the question of the identity of the New Testament. What is it about? Not in a thousand pages, but in a few—what is the New Testament about? What is its view of life?

Caird wrote:

> Literary and historical criticism, then, have made and are still making contributions to our understanding of the New Testament on which there is no going back. Yet the violent reaction with which these contributions were at first repudiated, and in some circles are still repudiated today, sprang from a sound if unenlightened instinct. Christian faith has always been nourished upon the word of Scripture, and could not indefinitely be satisfied with the disjecta membra of analytical scholarship. Sooner or later the demand was bound to be made for a new movement which should rediscover beneath the diversity the fundamental unity of the New Testament, which can be felt even by those who are unable to prove its existence. The prophet of the new movement was C. H. Dodd, who in his inaugural lecture at Cambridge in 1936 declared that the present task in New Testament studies was synthesis.[6]

Let me ask you something this morning, speaking neighbor to neighbor: Are we at a similar crossroads today in the study, in the reading, in the interpretation of the Bible? Have we, at least in some measure, invested such attention in the diversity and variety within the Scripture that we have left behind the marrow, the meaning, the heart, the theology of the whole?

Caird wrote, seventy years ago:

---

6. Caird, *New Testament View*, 7.

> The challenge of comparative religion has been honestly faced by Christian scholars, and in the long run it has served to confirm rather than to shake their confidence in the unique quality of their Scriptures. This confidence has been shown of late in a spate of books and articles whose purpose is to show how, without in any way sacrificing the gains of a century of criticism, we can still regard the Bible as the Word of God—a word communicated not by the automatic processes of verbal inspiration, but through the fallible powers and kaleidoscopic variety of human thought and speech, yet a word unique in its authority and appeal.[7]

Pause for a moment and savor Caird's language and imagery, his gracious rhetoric. Notice the words: unique . . . Word . . . kaleidoscopic variety . . . authority . . . appeal.

As we do, as we want to do, as we must do, we honor and with humility attend to the 250 years (and more, now) of historical-critical and other study of the Holy Scripture. Not to do so would be to deny the truth hard found, hard won, hard edged, of the historical study of Scripture, including its younger grandchildren and cousins now turning toward further varieties of lenses and modes of interpretation. Confronted with the possible dangers posed by such a conflagration, such a fire of investigation, Rudolph Bultmann wrote: "I calmly let the fire burn."[8] But at some point, there also arises—in fact, there arises as a consequence of all this labor—the abiding question of what it all means in a communicable, communal, contextual sense.

Caird continues:

> In the present state of New Testament studies, then, there is a growing disposition to emphasize both the unity and the uniqueness of the New Testament writings, though neither unity nor uniqueness can as yet be taken for granted. I propose, therefore, to set before you in three illustrations a view of life which seems to me to be common to all the richly varied writings of the New

---

7. Caird, *New Testament View*, 8.
8. Bultmann, *Faith and Understanding*, 132.

Testament and to be the peculiar contribution of those writings to the religious thought of mankind.[9]

So again let me ask you, speaking neighbor to neighbor: Are we at a similar crossroads today in the study, in the reading, in the interpretation of the Bible?

The Bible is not going anywhere; it is certainly not going away, particularly not away from the global mission, work, life and struggle of the church. This question of interpretation has become, for me, a deeply personal one. Within my beloved denomination, The United Methodist Church, our national and global inattention to a liberal biblical theology has contributed to a sorrowful, costly, and painful impasse and partial collapse.

So, in these following three sections, I first review Caird's own exploration of biblical theology from 1951 and then, hopefully in an accessible way, I enter the conversation here in 2022. I part company with Caird on many points, but I will honor his brief, at least in a slight and formal way, by borrowing his threefold outline for our exercise this morning.

His threefold outline, rephrased, is this: the New Testament presents a view of life that includes and celebrates *presence*—the presence of God, of the divine spirit in history, human history; a view of life that includes and celebrates the crucial *freedom* of the human being—sinners and saints and all in between; and a view of life that includes and celebrates that which we can learn in and through our own *experience*. Presence, freedom, and experience—these are unifying aspects of the New Testament fore and aft, across all its twenty-seven books, its manifold and maddening varieties, its contrary diversities, and its opaque and yet-not-fully mastered conundrums.

Let us, for a moment this morning, explore along these three paths in the exercise of a liberal biblical theology. We shall in each case begin with Caird, and then, in what Paul called the "partnership in the gospel,"[10] continue and advance with one or more

---

9. Caird, *New Testament View*, 8.
10. Phil 1:5, author's preferred translation.

partner voices (Ralph Harper, Samuel Terrien, Dietrich Bonhoeffer, Eric Fromm, Howard Thurman, Robert Frost, and others).

Caird grounded his work in the Trinity, in traditional Trinitarian language, as he took up his work on the unity of the New Testament. In some dissonance with what Caird wrote seventy years ago, I would like to use some more secular theological language to approach the biblical neighbor and neighborhood, especially and intentionally as we consider theological education in the twenty-first century.

III. Presence

Caird wrote, as was read on the floor of the library long ago, that the belief offered us by the New Testament "is a belief in God the Creator whose gracious favor embraces without respect of persons all the creatures of his handiwork. It is a belief in God the Redeemer who can turn darkness into light and whose reign is a saving reign. It is a belief in God the Spirit, through whose unremitting activity the reign of God is transmuted from an article of faith into a fact of experience."[11]

Put simply, it is the witness to belief in God—the witness to God—that gives the Bible in general its unity in the face of diversity.

Yet for some, perhaps for you, the three letters G-O-D may be more fence than doorway. Not only does the agnostic and the apophatic but also, and more so, does the average person—the "reasonable man" of insurance law—often stumble on those three letters. As the adage goes: "If God is God, he is not good, and if God is good, he is not God."[12] That is, it is hard to square concentric circles of love and power, of power and love.

This spring, ten thousand innocent civilians were slaughtered in Mariupol alone.[13] We are attuned to such suffering in part, let us confess, because those who died lived in homes like

11. Caird, *New Testament View*, 11.
12. MacLeish, "J. B.," 11.
13. Karmanau, Schreck, and Anna, "Mariupol."

AN INITIAL EXERCISE IN LIBERAL BIBLICAL THEOLOGY

those we live in. They shopped in stores resembling our own. They used social media and the internet, as do you. They rode transit, owned cars, vacationed in Barcelona, spoke multiple languages, and tragically became part of a new or renewed appetite for slaughter on the part of the Russian government. If God could stop that and didn't, he is not good. If God would stop it and couldn't, he is not God. For some, hence, the three letters, G-O-D, are more fence than doorway.

Nor does it help that our halting, partial overtures to a sound, liberal, biblical theology have sometimes shorn us, the people of faith, of our vocabulary. Sin? We hardly name it. Death? We rarely face it. The daily threat of meaningless? We barely conceive it. And then, in the democracy just south of here, along comes a six-year political crisis, including January 6th. And then along comes a two- or three-year hibernation in the Covid cave. And then along comes the invasion of Ukraine, with a whiff of nuclear bombast—nuclear bomb blast—in the air. Creation can be seen; salvation can be felt. But fall? The fallenness of creation? The abject, dire need, one beggar telling another where both can find bread, the impossible possibility in fallenness ... of salvation? We were absent that day, or we took another course—not that there is any. Or, we thought, we had bigger fish to fry—not that there are any. In these times, we can see the need for a sound, gracious, liberal biblical theology. Sin is the absence of God. Death is the absence of God. Meaninglessness is the absence of God. But you, it may well be, are not at ease with those three letters, G-O-D. They seem a fancy, a fiction, an antique mistake.

Sometimes they seem so to me, too—though, in fact and in full, I hold fast to the ancient traditions and language. Sometimes they seem so to me given our current cultural, linguistic incapacity for—our cultural, linguistic exclusion of—the three letters, G-O-D. The Scriptures offer, however, a gift, a saving one: another three words that mean G-O-D but that may better say so, at least for some, for a time, in our time. *Presence* and *freedom* and *experience*: a back porch entry, not a front porch one. Today you may find wonder, marvel, and amazement ... just here.

Now let me turn from "God the Creator" to the simpler, yet fully biblical, word "presence," from Caird to Harper.

One summer some years ago, our family went on a three-day trip to Maine. We stopped in Kennebunkport and swam in the ocean. That day the newspaper carried a review of a short book called *On Presence*. The book had been written by Ralph Harper, a then unknown Episcopal priest in Maryland, and it had won a prestigious prize. I remember feeling struck by Harper's reflection on the difficulty of writing honestly after preaching nearly every Sunday for more than two decades, as he had. I stuffed the review in my shirt pocket and bought the book (albeit nine months later). The book is about presence, the sense of presence, and the practice of the presence of God. It is about being amazed.

Harper wrote: "We have too short a time on this earth to pass up any chance to find words and images to live by. I believe almost everyone is capable of being moved by some person, place, nature, or individual work of art. Of course, there is instability and incoherence in and about us all the time. There is also an inexhaustible store of Being to keep us permanently in awe."[14]

He went on: "Not everything can be said easily, except claims of absolute affirmation or denial. In time most things can be said clearly, at least. And some of these things are so important that we should do everything we can to make them clear. Presence is one of these things. It is not a word that we should allow anyone to rule out of our vocabulary and discourse."[15]

Here is a footnote to a sense of presence. At Union Theological Seminary, Samuel Terrien (whose widow, Sarah, graciously phoned me my first autumn in Boston) taught us, in melodious prose, that "in biblical faith, presence eludes, but does not delude."[16] Terrien wrote: "God is near, but his presence remains elusive."[17] His is the elusive presence of a walking, not a

---

14. Harper, *On Presence*, viii.
15. Harper, *On Presence*, 119.
16. Terrien, *Elusive Presence*, 476.
17. Terrien, *Elusive Presence*, 170.

sitting, God;[18] a God of tent, not temple;[19] of ear, not eye;[20] of name, not glory;[21] a God of time, not space;[22] of grace, not place, in whom does our faith allow us to translate love for God into actual behavior in society.[23] "Presence does not alter nature but it changes history through the character of [human beings]."[24]

IV. Freedom

Caird, in his essay, looked hard at the matter of redemption, of God as Redeemer. This is the gospel of the God who is loving us into love and freeing us into freedom, the God whose love gives us freedom and makes a way for freedom. Caird wrote:

> Still more important is the answer which the New Testament gives to the problem of evil. To the academic question, "What is the origin of evil?" the New Testament indeed neither gives nor attempts to give an answer: nor do I believe that any consistent theory can be propounded by the finite mind of man which will not do violence to some of the facts of experience. But to the practical questions, "Why does not God do something about evil?" and "What can we do about the evil that confronts us?" the New Testament has a fully satisfying reply. God has done something. His kingdom of righteousness has broken in upon the kingdom of Satan to set free those who were held in bondage to evil habits and evil institutions. "If I by the finger of God cast out demons, then without doubt the kingdom of God has come upon you." He has "called us out of darkness into his marvelous light." In the decisive battle of Calvary the serried ranks of evil have been defeated by Jesus' calm obedience to the

18. Terrien, *Elusive Presence*, 170–1.
19. Terrien, *Elusive Presence*, 179.
20. Terrien, *Elusive Presence*, 112; 201.
21. Terrien, *Elusive Presence*, 138.
22. Terrien, *Elusive Presence*, 186.
23. Terrien, *Elusive Presence*, 201.
24. Terrien, *Elusive Presence*, 235.

will of God, and men may now join him in the victorious campaign in which every enemy is to be put under his feet. "Thanks be to God who gives us the victory!"[25]

Now let me turn from "God the Redeemer" to the different, yet fully biblical, word "freedom," from Caird to Bonhoeffer (and a few of his cousins).

During my first year of study at Union Theological Seminary, I lived on the second floor of Hastings Hall in the room that had, decades earlier, been inhabited by Dietrich Bonhoeffer. In 1934, Bonhoeffer had declared that "the church that calls a people to belief in Christ must itself be, in the midst of that people, the burning fire of love, the nucleus of reconciliation, the source of the fire in which all hate is smothered and proud, hateful people are transformed into loving people."[26]

Bonhoeffer joins some of the greatest voices in our tradition in steadily connecting redemption and freedom, in ways that fill out the meaning of both. "To act out of concrete responsibility," Bonhoeffer wrote, "means to act in *freedom*—to decide, to act, and to answer for the consequences of this particular action *myself* without the support of other people or principles. Responsibility presupposes ultimate freedom in assessing a given situation, in choosing, and in acting."[27] Then: "Precisely because we are dealing with a deed that arises from freedom, the one who acts is not torn apart by destructive conflict, but instead can with confidence and inner integrity do the unspeakable, namely, in the very act of breaking the law to sanctify it."[28]

Paul Tillich emphasized the power of participation—in discussions about the truth of faith, in the experience of faith, in the community of faith—and the freedom expressed by such participation.[29] Others have made similar or related claims, claims that render redemption in the language of freedom.

25. Caird, *New Testament View*, 10.
26. Bonhoeffer, *London*, 392.
27. Bonhoeffer, *Ethics*, 221. (Emphasis in the original.)
28. Bonhoeffer, *Ethics*, 297.
29. See, for example: Tillich, *Systematic Theology, Vol. 3*, 129–38; 231–45.

In such freedom did Dr. Douglas John Hall, our esteemed, beloved teacher here at McGill and a onetime student of Tillich, impress upon me that ours is a religion that must share spiritual nurture of the world with many other faith traditions.

In such freedom did Bishop Michael Curry say, during the upheaval in the Episcopal Church following Gene Robinson's election to the office of bishop:

> I noticed something. While some people were upset and expressing that, the majority were supportive or politely silent. There is very often a sensible center, a silent or quiet majority who are being drowned out by the loudest, most extreme voices. But they are there. Many are simply waiting for the angry to exhaust themselves. They listen patiently, waiting for a deeper wisdom to emerge.
>
> Something else happened with some regularity. Quietly a parent would whisper in my ear, "Thank you." They would tell me that their son or daughter, niece or nephew, was gay. This happened regularly.[30]

In such freedom did our colleague Ibram X. Kendi say, in a lecture recently given at Boston University: "Racist power is not godly. Racist policies are not indestructible. Racial inequities are not inevitable. Racist ideas are not natural to the human mind.... Once we lose hope, we are guaranteed to lose."[31]

Here is a footnote to a sense of freedom. Erich Fromm warned us about the dread of freedom; he traced the effects on freedom that result from the lack of hope; he pointed to the daily effects of such. Ultimately, Fromm offered a clear, divine word of hope, both in and for freedom: "*Positive freedom consists in the spontaneous activity of the total, integrated personality,*"[32] he wrote. "*There is only one meaning of life: the act of living itself.*"[33] "By one course [the individual] can progress to 'positive freedom'; he can relate himself spontaneously to the world in love

---

30. Curry and Grace, *Love is the Way*, 180–1.
31. Kendi, *How to Be an Antiracist*, 238.
32. Fromm, *Escape from Freedom*, 258. (Emphasis in the original.)
33. Fromm, *Escape from Freedom*, 263. (Emphasis in the original.)

and work, in the genuine expression of his emotional, sensuous, and intellectual capacities; he can thus become one again with man, nature, and himself, without giving up the independence and integrity of his individual self."[34]

Spontaneity! Camaraderie! Emotion! Intellect! Where you come alongside these, according to Fromm's work, there, we might say, is freedom.

V. Experience

Experience, Caird reminded us, is the foundation for our beliefs, for our actions, for our very personhood. "Christians were united in a common experience before ever they agreed to explain that experience in a common doctrine," he wrote. "The whole Christian movement began with something that happened to a small group of men and women, and it continued and grew because by their testimony they were able to share with others their experience."[35]

In speaking broadly of God the Sustainer, Caird gave us a framework for our engagement in the experiences of this world:

> The Christian who knows and practices the New Testament faith regards the world not as a vale of tears or as a house of correction, but as a fit setting for a life of heavenly citizenship. He engages in good works and social reforms, not because he has an illusory belief in progress, but because love to one's neighbor is the law of the city to which he belongs. Yet he escapes the lures of materialism and worldliness through the knowledge that his ultimate allegiance is to a city whose builder and maker is God.[36]

Interpreted through such a frame, events of an individual past reveal meaning and fold into the conscious past of our community and of humankind. Study of theology can aid our understanding of, though never substitute for, lived experience.

---

34. Fromm, *Escape from Freedom*, 140.
35. Caird, *New Testament View*, 13.
36. Caird, *New Testament View*, 12.

"To study the theological terminology of the New Testament is to see the new wine of experience burst one after another of the old bottles of language and thought. And it is no criticism of St. Paul as a theologian if we say that he touches the deepest springs of our spiritual life when the theologian yields to the poet,"[37] Caird wrote. "The science of theology must be subservient to the practice of Christian living."[38]

Invoking the metaphor offered by Hebrews 12:1, Caird reminded us that our single thread of experience will weave into a greater tapestry. "The saints of the past have run their lap and carried the baton of faith successfully to the end of the course. Now they throng the seats of the stadium to watch a new generation run in its turn.... Perfection is a social achievement, and only in the corporate perfection of the new society of God's kingdom can a man find his own subordinate perfection."[39]

Still later, Caird continued:

> To the *fatalism* of those who see the world hustled by a blind impulse to an unknown destiny the New Testament proclaims that behind the manifold workings of the mysterious universe there is a personal and purposing power: to the *loneliness* of those whom the friendship of this world has failed to satisfy, it offers the fellowship of a new society; to the *optimism* which still hopes to build utopia by social reform it declares that that society is already in being; to the *materialism* which has submitted to the facile attractions of worldly security and comfort it asserts that the kingdom is not of this world; to the *rationalism* which demands logical proof it responds with the testimony of personal experience; and to the *pessimism* which is overwhelmed by the burden of the world's shame and sorrow it gives the assurance that the Lord God omnipotent reigns.[40]

---

37. Caird, *New Testament View*, 13.
38. Caird, *New Testament View*, 14.
39. Caird, *New Testament View*, 13.
40. Caird, *New Testament View*, 14. (All emphasis mine.)

Now let me turn from "God the Sustainer" to the simpler, yet fully biblical, word "experience," from Caird to Thurman.

In thinking of experience, take my beloved predecessor as Dean of Marsh Chapel, Howard Thurman—a poetic theologian, and a theological poet, one who celebrated experience. He was a hundred years ahead of his time when he sat at my own desk (from 1953 to 1965), so he is still fifty years ahead of me! As Thurman would emphasize, our experience teaches us. He recalled late-night walks along his beloved Daytona Beach, alone and with his feet in the sand: "The ocean and the night together surrounded my little life with a reassurance that could not be affronted by the behavior of human beings. The ocean at night gave me a sense of timelessness, of existing beyond the reach of the ebb and flow of circumstances. Death would be a minor thing, I felt, in the sweep of that natural embrace."[41]

It happened that, this spring at Boston University, a wonderful, beloved, seventy-five-year-old professor died in mid lecture. Later, the fifteen students from the class were gathered. After initial awkwardness, they began to speak, and a full *presence* filled the room. One spoke a soliloquy on trauma and grief. One gave a soliloquy on connection in hardship. One spoke a soliloquy on pride and love. One gave a soliloquy on how others—the professor's faculty friends, who had known him so much longer—might be hurting so much more. Then, a moment: "Let's go visit them and offer our condolences," one said. And they did. It was a powerful, poetic moment—an experience. Where did we ever get the idea that twenty-year-olds cannot say and do great things?

Dean Thurman was a lover of the Psalms. Presence, his sense of presence, his practice of presence, intimate to the natural world, led him to such love. To know Howard Thurman was to share his experience in worship, sacrament, prayer, singing, spirituals, preaching—and in religion. He had a favorite Psalm or two; perhaps you do as well. Pick two and learn them by heart this year. Maybe this week, you will read one in this setting, this beautiful chapel at McGill University; maybe you will, like so

---

41. Thurman, *With Head and Heart*, 8.

many others have in this place, find, and be found by, presence. Start, perhaps, with Psalm 139:

> Where can I go from your spirit?
> Or where can I flee from your presence?
> If I ascend to heaven, you are there;
> if I make my bed in Sheol, you are there.
> If I take the wings of the morning
> and settle at the farthest limits of the sea,
> even there your hand shall lead me,
> and your right hand shall hold me fast.
> If I say, "Surely the darkness shall cover me,
> and the light around me become night,"
> even the darkness is not dark to you;
> the night is as bright as the day,
> for darkness is as light to you.[42]

For Howard Thurman, presence—the experience of presence—is a central word for God, perhaps the central word for God. Here we find another back porch entry, instead of a front porch one. Like Thurman, and like the Psalmist held fast even in the dark of night, you may find wonder, marvel, and amazement in presence. For, as we have learned, "in thy presence is fullness of joy."[43]

Here is a footnote to a sense of experience. The New England poet Robert Frost beautifully honored our experience in so many of his dark, dour poems, including (speaking of crossing the border) this famous one set against the border:

> *I Could Give All To Time*
>
> To Time it never seems that he is brave
> To set himself against the peaks of snow
> To lay them level with the running wave,
> Nor is he overjoyed when they lie low,
> But only grave, contemplative and grave.

---

42. Ps 139:7–12, NRSV.
43. Ps 16:1, KJV.

> What now is inland shall be ocean isle,
> Then eddies playing round a sunken reef
> Like the curl at the corner of a smile;
> And I could share Time's lack of joy or grief
> At such a planetary change of style.
> I could give all to Time except—except
> What I myself have held. But why declare
> The things forbidden that while the Customs slept
> I have crossed to Safety with? For I am There,
> And what I would not part with I have kept.[44]

Frost's own engagement with the Christian tradition is itself a complex story that would take us several hours of labor to unwind. But with these words, he came quite close to the emphasis on experience that is a hallmark of centrality, of unity in diversity, within the fullness of the Scripture.

VI. Coda

I am grateful to have had your attention over these past fifty minutes and six thousand words, during which my intention has been to engage us in an exercise in liberal biblical theology that may serve into the future as an example for such conversation among neighbors within and alongside the global church. One exercise, toward which leans the partnership in the Gospel, may be found in both academic and religious reflection on these cognates to the divine: *presence, freedom, experience*. Are there other such cognates? For sure. Start your list. Yet when we are in Scripture, are we ever very far from presence (or its shadow, absence), from freedom (or its shadow, bondage), or from experience (or its shadow, loneliness)? I think not.

For those who may think, rightly, that I have spoken for a long time without quoting much Scripture, here are some

---

44. Frost, *Complete Poems*, 334–5.

AN INITIAL EXERCISE IN LIBERAL BIBLICAL THEOLOGY

Scriptural signposts toward presence, freedom, and experience as found in the letter to the Galatians:

"I have been crucified with Christ; and it is no longer I who live, but it is Christ who lives in me. And the life I now live in the flesh I live by faith in the Son of God, who loved me and gave himself for me."[45] *Presence: I live by.*

"For freedom Christ has set us free. Stand firm, therefore, and do not submit again to a yoke of slavery."[46] *Freedom: set free.*

"By contrast, the fruit of the Spirit is love, joy, peace, patience, kindness, generosity, faithfulness, gentleness, and self-control. There is no law against such things."[47] *Experience: fruit.*

Some friendly theological signposts on the road toward liberal biblical theology include these following, from James Sanders and John Collins. Said Sanders: "[Scriptural canon] functions, for the most part, to provide indications of the identity as well as the life-style of the on-going community which reads it."[48] "The primary characteristic of canon . . . is its adaptability."[49] "Adaptability and stability. That is canon. Each generation reads its authoritative tradition in the light of its own place in life, its own questions, its own necessary hermeneutics. This is inevitable. Around this core were gathered many other materials, as time went on, adaptable to it."[50]

Said John J. Collins: "Whether or not one can conceive of a biblical theology grounded in historical criticism obviously depends on whether one insists on a faith commitment that exempts some positions from criticism, or whether one is willing to regard biblical theology as an extension of the critical enterprise that deals with truth-claims and values in an open-ended engagement with the text."[51] Later: "The discovery of structural unity

---

45. Gal 2:19–20, NRSV.
46. Gal 5:1, NRSV.
47. Gal 5:22–23, NRSV.
48. Sanders, "Adaptable for Life," 537.
49. Sanders, "Adaptable for Life," 539.
50. Sanders, "Adaptable for Life," 551.
51. Collins, *Encounters with Biblical Theology*, 3.

PARTNERSHIP IN THE GOSPEL

in a tradition that spans a millennium has also proven endlessly problematic from a historical point of view."[52]

Says Robert Allan Hill: I am a Liberal—in theology, Paul Tillich; in philosophy, Isaiah Berlin; in culture, Marilynn Robinson; in economics, Paul Krugman; in politics, Barack Obama. I am Liberal, not orthodox, fundamentalist, conservative, or traditionalist; but I am also Liberal, not progressivist, successivist, anarchist, liberationist, or Marxist.

Finally, by way of encouragement, Pasternak always ended with Shakespeare's 66th, so we shall, too.

> Tired with all these, for restful death I cry,
> As, to behold desert a beggar born,
> And needy nothing trimm'd in jollity,
> And purest faith unhappily forsworn,
> And gilded honour shamefully misplaced,
> And maiden virtue rudely strumpeted,
> And right perfection wrongfully disgraced,
> And strength by limping sway disabled,
> And art made tongue-tied by authority,
> And folly doctor-like controlling skill,
> And simple truth miscall'd simplicity,
> And captive good attending captain ill:
> Tired with all these, from these would I be gone,
> Save that, to die, I leave my love alone.[53]

---

52. Collins, *Encounters with Biblical Theology*, 13.
53. Shakespeare, "66," 1036.

2

"No Male and Female": Ruminations on the New Creation

THE CURRENT TROUBLE AND dilemma for The UMC lies in its reckoning with *missio Dei* in our time and for our connectional situation—which is to say, in the midst of our time's struggle to prioritize human rights, and for a church that has fallen out of sync with the needs of its community. Why we in The UMC can allow latitude regarding issues of life and death, abortion and warfare, but cannot allow such latitude regarding love and marriage is a mystery and truly says much about the remains of the mind of the church.

This task deserves and requires a comparative exploration of the ancient, Pauline vision of the new creation. The gospel of new creation, as Theodore Runyon explained, moves sanctification toward the renewal of all creation: "The cosmic drama of the renewing of creation begins . . . with the renewal of the *imago Dei* in humankind."[1]

Within such an exploration of the new creation readily arises the gospel affirmation of the full inclusion of gay people

---

1. Runyon, *New Creation*, 12.

within the Body of Christ. We heed Paul, whose writing of the new creation in Galatians proclaims that all of our present-age distinctions—religious, ethnic, socioeconomic, and gender—are nothing. We notice the difference between old traditions and new-creational traditions, and we question the division between peoples based on sexuality—the dehumanization based on sex—founded on antiquated models rather than on the theology of the new creation. We hear and acknowledge the experiences of friends and relatives—siblings in Christ—who are gay.

Finally—having a Scriptural and theological basis for the acceptance of gay people, and having experienced the pain, of our neighbors and ourselves, induced by a categorical rejection of certain of God's children—we reason that there must be another way to think about faith, another way to think about that which unites us. Our duty in the new creation, as Runyon would have it, is to live in connection and in service to all: "Salvation consists . . . not only in reconciliation but in service, not only in an experienced sense of God's reality and presence but in a life lived out of that reality, extending divine transforming power into every aspect of both individual and social existence."[2] What reasonable ways forward can we find to live the vision of the new creation, of *missio Dei*, here on earth?

With this in mind, this chapter follows a trajectory from pastoral experience to scriptural interpretation to theological traditions to reasoned debate. Forty years of pastoral ministry carry the content of the rumination in the first section. Scriptural interpretation, exegesis, and exposition of Galatians, both generally and of Galatians 3:28 in particular, and with reliance on one of the best modern commentaries on Galatians, grounds the second section. The Wesley quadrilateral, applied to traditions in theological reflection, shapes the third section. Following experience, scripture, and tradition, the last section offers a reasoned debate and discussion of a collection of essays called *Finding Our Way: Love and Law in The United Methodist Church*. At the end of it all, we shall find that the biblical gospel, under

2. Runyon, *New Creation*, 12.

the aspect and aegis of a liberal biblical theology, and as shown through experience, tradition, Scripture, and reason, affirms the full humanity of gay people.

Versions and portions of this chapter have been presented in print,[3] in lecture,[4] in seminar setting denominational debate,[5] in the pulpit,[6] and in classroom lecture and discussion.[7]

I. Pastoral Experience

I am grateful for the magnanimous, loving people we have known in the experience of pastoral ministry, who have embodied and awaited the new creation.

In late August of 2017, my wife Jan and I went to London to celebrate our fortieth wedding anniversary. Though we had not been there for several years, the memories and ghosts of earlier visits quickened once we landed. We had taken a church group through London in 2000, and I remembered how Jane Amey and her husband Bill, both in their mid-eighties, had struggled to move their luggage along through customs. I could feel Jane alongside us in customs again.

Jane sang in the choir; she led in the service ministry; she volunteered to answer the office phone. In her early years she had ridden along with her mother to Methodist gatherings in New Jersey, to sort out the shape of the WSCS.[8] She remembered the mission work in China before it ended. When asked about her service, her

---

3. Originally published in a slightly different form in *Missio Dei and the United States: Toward a Faithful United Methodist Witness* (Nashville: General Board of Higher Education and Ministry, The United Methodist Church, 2018), 103–19. Reprinted by permission of the author and the publisher.

4. SMU Perkins School of Theology, August 2019.

5. Boston United Methodist Church, November 2018.

6. Various; especially First United Methodist Church, San Diego, February 2020.

7. Various; especially Boston University School of Theology.

8. Women's Society for Christian Service was what The United Methodist Church called United Methodist Women at the time.

giving, her happy singing, and her faith, she invariably said: "We just don't want to leave anyone behind."

That was her way of speaking about *missio Dei*, the divine inclusive incursion into the orb of the human condition, by way of the guidance to leave no one behind. She very much meant, by the way, to include gay people in the loving evangelism and stewardship of the church, in its own frail attempts to live into *missio Dei*. We just don't want to leave anyone behind.

Back in London, having passed through customs and settled into a hotel near Westminster, other ghosts and memories emerged. Past my mind's eye sauntered Bishop Ralph Ward, our long-dead General Superintendent, who in 1972 took a group of us to London and into the Abbey. Ralph showed us the Methodist sites and arranged for us a dinner at Methodist Central Hall, which had, after the Second World War, hosted the birth of the United Nations. The superintending minister of Central Hall spoke of the War and moved us, moved us to tears, even those of us only seventeen at the time.

Jan and I worshipped at Westminster Abbey, our feet resting on the memorial to William Wilberforce, and then crossed the street to see Central Hall again. By the late 1970s, Ralph Ward had moved to New York City and gathered some of us local seminarians at Washington Square UMC one Friday evening to support ministry with gay people. His Manhattan District Superintendent, Bernie Kirkland, presided with grace and love: *this work is crucial to the life of the church,* he expressed.

Some years later, after his retirement, Jan and I saw Ralph and his wife Arleen in the narthex of Riverside Church, after worship which that day had concluded with the singing of "Love Divine, All Loves Excelling." We sang that same hymn at the funeral of Arlene Chapman in Watertown, New York. Her husband Bruce, along with my dad, took me at age eight to my first major-league baseball game in Cooperstown, New York. (The two last-place teams in professional baseball were conscripted to play upstate once a year, as punishment for their losing ways. One of the teams was, of course, the Mets.) Driving home, I foolishly waved my new

Mets hat at a passerby on Route 20. The wind blew it away. But Bruce turned the car around and we found the thing.

Some years later, Bruce would speak, quietly and gently, into the microphone at The UMC Annual Conference: *In 1980 and 1984, I was a General Conference delegate. I, and others, opposed the inclusion of gay people in orders and marriage. How utterly wrong I was. How foolishly wrong we were.*

A graduate of Boston University before studying at Yale Divinity, Bruce still supports BU through an annual gift to Marsh Chapel. Marsh Chapel, after its construction was completed in 1949, welcomed Tom Trotter as its first speaker. Tom's grandson would later become an intern at the same chapel. Both Bruce and Tom were at BU during the Thurman and King Jr. years. As a pastor, Bruce could tell you what every pastor knows who has at least five years of good working experience: every extended family system, in Methodism and beyond, has at least one gay person somewhere in it. I asked Bruce what he, after his own sixty years of experience, would teach seminarians about ministry. *Stay close to your people*, he said.

Jan and I have had the honor to serve in ten churches, one district, one University pulpit, and several general church efforts, including one in Boston 2017, all focused on *missio Dei*. Every congregation we have served has had gay women and men in it, or in the extended families therein. That any of these good people have stayed at all in connection with our connection, given our exclusion of them from *missio Dei*, is a wonder.

I love my church and am staying with it—born and baptized a Methodist, I will so die and be buried. I am not giving over the church I love to a mode of exclusion contrary to the heart of the church in which I have lived and served. But we should be mightily circumspect about what bigotry against gay people has already done—to us, the body of The UMC.

This topic has many facets, and I will pass many of them over, which is not meant to say that they are any less worthy of discussion in another arena. I pass over the innumerable women and men who have left ours for ordination in other denominations. I pass over the hurt to evangelism and stewardship that comes with ribald exclusionary doctrine. I pass over the diminishment of membership, particularly in the congregations of the northern US and the extended north, due to young adults, especially millennials, who sense the homophobia in our sanctuaries and find another place. This is a spiritual issue, not one of numbers. It is a theological issue, not one of members. It is a biblical issue, not one of congregations. It is a homiletical issue, not one of disciplinary interpretation. This cuts to, and cuts into, our soul.

Here is what I mean: gay people are people, but we preach otherwise. God loves gay people, but we teach otherwise. In Christ, "there is no male and female,"[9] but we argue otherwise. Such spiritual, theological, biblical, and homiletical malignancy and mendacity is crippling us.

A lifetime in pastoral ministry has provided Jan and me with many snapshots of grace touching the lives of gay people, that grace being the beachhead of God's incursion into life:

Here is a novice pastor in the rough, poor, rural upstate New York border country in 1982, and with him, talking slowly in the February snow, is a young man, age nineteen, realizing his identity, struggling with his family, his church, and himself.

Here is that same pastor in the autumn of 1991, a bit older, attending a community dinner in his city neighborhood, seated with eight women—no, he then dimly realizes, seated with four bright, happy, earnest, loving couples.

Here is the pastor in 2004, calling on a recently-retired schoolteacher and her partner—both longtime and long-suffering servants of God and neighbor, and members of a United Methodist church—and listening as they cry and cry out in bitterness over the ignorance and exclusion they have known in a large, supposedly-accepting city church.

Here he is in 2008 as minister of the gospel, new to deanship, employing and deploying an openly gay campus minister to serve across a large University campus, one that, despite its

---

9. Gal 3:28, NRSV.

liberal history and spirit, had until then never hired such a person for such a position.

And here he is, in September of 2017, offering prayers at the Boston University School of Public Health: prayers for those who, thirty years earlier, had died of AIDS—often without willing pastoral care from their churches—and prayers for those who ministered to them.

To put a fine point on it: any pastor who has done the minimum two dozen or so weekly visits over a few years knows full well that every family system, near or far, includes gay people within it. This issue in relation to *missio Dei* is not somehow *out there*, far away, foreign, peripheral, or minimal. It is immediate, ongoing, and unavoidable.

Unresolved, the issue will pulverize the church. *Missio Dei*, the mission of God, the sending of God, the preaching of the gospel of "Jesus Christ, and him crucified,"[10] starts with God's love for all. A preliminary incision to curtail the divine love, and thus the *missio Dei*, by excluding, dehumanizing, and imprisoning gay people in a pseudo-biblical jail constitutes the articulation of another gospel—not that there is any other gospel.

II. Scriptural Interpretation

Every generation comes afresh upon the strange world of the Bible. Paul's letter to the churches of Galatia, from the late 40s or 50s of the first century, may open for us some new and truly remarkable insights especially fit for those in United Methodist ministry today.

This fiery letter, Paul's writing at the outset of the mission to the Gentiles, has sparked and attended much debate over the course of history: at the creation of the New Testament (Marcion); at the dawn of the Reformation ("it is my Katie von Bora")[11]; in

---

10. 1 Cor 2:2, NRSV.

11. Luther, *Luther's Works*, 26:ix. Luther's description of the letter to the Galatians as "my Katie von Bora," a reference to his own beloved wife, indicated the strength of his connection to the letter.

the Wesleyan movement ("finish then thy new creation")[12]; in the heart of the US Civil Rights movement ("I bear in my body the marks of the Lord Jesus").[13]

In the context of this and other of Paul's letters, J. Louis Martyn argues that "the apostle was aware of the fact that even in the church, the beachhead of God's new creation, there were as yet some marks of sexual and social differentiation (eg. 1 Cor 7; Philemon). He had later therefore to think very seriously about the tension between the affirmation of real unity in Christ and the disconcerting continuation of the distinguishing marks of the old creation. In writing to the Galatians he does not pause over that matter."[14]

Consider the letter's key sentences:

"I received [the gospel] through a revelation of Jesus Christ."[15] *Revelation: apocalypse.*

"I have been crucified with Christ; and it is no longer I who live, but it is Christ who lives in me. And the life I now live in the flesh I live by the faith of the Son of God who loved me and gave himself for me."[16]

"In Christ Jesus you are all children of God through faith. As many of you as were baptized into Christ have clothed yourselves with Christ. There is no longer Jew or Greek, there is no longer slave or free, there is no longer male and female; for all of you are one in Christ Jesus. And if you belong to Christ, then you are Abraham's offspring, heirs according to the promise."[17]

"For freedom Christ has set us free. Stand firm, therefore, and do not submit again to a yoke of slavery."[18]

"May I never boast of anything except the cross of our Lord Jesus Christ, by which the world has been crucified to me, and I

---

12. Wesley and Wesley, *Collection of Hymns*, 281.

13. King Jr., *Letter from Birmingham City Jail*, 10. This quote from King Jr. is Gal 6:17.

14. Martyn, *Galatians*, 377.

15. Gal 1:12, NRSV.

16. Gal 2:19–220e, NRSV.

17. Gal 3:26–28, NRSV.

18. Gal 5:1, NRSV.

to the world. For neither circumcision nor uncircumcision is anything; but a new creation is everything!"[19]

When these theme sentences from Galatians—"the Magna Carta of Christian liberty"[20]—are read seriatim, steadily, and in a spirited mode, one hears something entirely new. The new is the very *missio Dei*. "Instead of being the holy community that stands apart from the profane orb of the world, then, the church is the beachhead God is planting in his war of liberation from all religious differentiations," Martyn writes. "The distinction between church and world is in nature apocalyptic rather than religious. . . . A significant commentary on Paul's letters can be found in the remark of Dietrich Bonhoeffer that 'God has founded his church beyond religion.'"[21]

1. Exposition

J. Louis Martyn's subtle, apocalyptic interpretation of Galatians has inspired many of us for decades, and it is here, in the course of rumination upon the new creation, to which we turn.

What does Galatians 3:28 offer us, here and now? In this passage, Paul makes use of a pre-Pauline baptismal formula, which he then interprets. Martyn notes that Paul intentionally recites and rejects Genesis 1:27 ("So God created humankind in his image, in the image of God he created them; male and female he created them.") The wording of the sentence's final clause differs from that of the previous two clauses, argues Martyn, signaling an intentional, didactic reference to Genesis 1:27 and "thereby saying that in baptism the structure of the original creation had been set aside."[22] Baptism, says Martyn, "is a participation both in Christ's death and in Christ's life; for genuine, eschatological life commences when one is taken into the community

---

19. Gal 6:14–15, NRSV.
20. See, for example: Luther, *Luther's Works*, 26:ix.
21. Martyn, *Galatians*, 37.
22. Martyn, *Galatians*, 376.

of the new creation in which unity in God's Christ has replaced religious-ethnic differentiation. In a word, religious and ethnic differentiations and that which underlies them—the Law—are identified in effect as 'the old things' that have now 'passed away,' giving place to the new creation (2 Cor 5:17)."[23]

In the apocalyptic *now* of the New Person of Christ—that is, in full reality—the oppositions between religious and unreligious, rich and poor, male and female, no longer exist. In Galatians, Paul teaches not of creation, but of new creation. He intentionally, sharply, and harshly contrasts the former—the creation which is, in reality, non-creation—with the latter, the new creation. Martyn explains:

> The traditions about Jesus find him arguing both on the basis of creation and on the basis of the gospel's power to bring about a new creation—the eschatological family—and between these two kinds of arguments there is a discernible tension.
>
> One can sense a similar tension in Paul's letters, *if* one takes them as a whole. In Rom 1:18–32 Paul uses an argument explicitly based on creation, drawing certain conclusions from "the things [God] has made" in "the creation of the cosmos" (Rom 1:20). In effect, Paul says in this passage that God's identity and the true sexual identity of human beings as male and female can both be inferred from creation.
>
> What a different argument lies before us in Gal 3:26–29; 6:14–15! Here the basis is explicitly not creation, but rather the new creation in which the building blocks of the old creation are declared to be nonexistent.[24]

Refer to Galatians 6:15–16: "For neither circumcision nor uncircumcision is anything; but a new creation is everything! As for those who will follow this rule—peace be upon them, and mercy, and upon the Israel of God."

Martyn continues:

---

23. Martyn, *Galatians*, 382–3.
24. Martyn, *Galatians*, 381. (Emphasis in the original.)

> If one were to recall the affirmation "It is not good that the man should be alone" (Gen 2:18), one would also remember that the creational response to loneliness is married fidelity between man and woman (Gen 2:24; Mark 10:6–7). But in its announcement of the new creation, the apocalyptic baptismal formula declares the erasure of the distinction of male from female. Now the answer to loneliness is not marriage, but rather the new-creational community that God is calling into being in Christ, the church marked by mutual love, as it is led by the Spirit of Christ. . . .
>
> The result of such a radical vision and of its radical argumentation is the new-creational view of the people of God. . . . It is Christ and the community of those incorporated into him who lie beyond religious distinctions.[25]

Paul's Epistle to the Galatians is one of the high peaks of the New Testament. It is about a whole new life, a new creation, in which there is freedom from those religious, ethnic, socioeconomic, and gender distinctions that divide us. There is a singular, awesome freedom in the way Paul understands new life in Christ. And yet, in the church that bears His name, we have yet to acknowledge in full that freedom.

The letter is written to address this question: *Must a Gentile become a Jew before he can become a Christian?* Is there a religious condition to be met, prior to the reception of God's apocalypse in Christ?

Paul was converted to Christ, as he says earlier in this letter, "by apocalypse." Christ revealed himself to Paul. Thus, for Paul, the authority in Christ is not finally in the Scripture, nor in traditions, nor in reason, nor in experience. Christ captured Paul through none of these, but rather through revelation, the apocalypse of God.

After Paul had been converted to Christ, he spent seventeen years in unremarkable, quiet ministry in Arabia. We know nothing of this time, but we have, in Galatians 2, a record of what happened

---

25. Martyn, *Galatians*, 381–2.

next: after these seventeen years, Paul traveled to Jerusalem to meet with the pillars of the church.

Can you picture the moment? All in one room: Paul, Peter, James, John. And in that room, there was argument, difference. Paul preached the cross of Christ to people unreligious from a Jewish perspective, and the unreligious—the uncircumcised—heard. What would the Jerusalem elders say? Jesus was a Jew, and had been circumcised. So, also, were all the first Christians, including Paul himself.

But God had done something astounding. It was the Gentiles, not the Jews, who fervently believed the Good News. Should these unreligious children of God be brought back into the Covenant of Circumcision? No, they all agreed, no. God had done something new. So, Peter went to the circumcised, and Paul went to the uncircumcised. Peter went to the Jews, and Paul to the Gentiles. They agreed to disagree, agreeably. And the meeting ended and it was settled. The freedom of the gospel trumped the ordered inheritance of tradition.

But have you ever noticed that sometimes it's not the meeting that counts, but the meeting after the meeting? What was settled in Jerusalem was unsettled a short time after. Peter couldn't be counted on to hold the line, and Paul told him as much: Peter was inconsistent in his use of freedom—sometimes he ate with the unclean Gentiles, and sometimes, when somebody was watching, he backed away. Paul, perceiving these inconsistencies, "opposed him to his face,"[26] not talking *about* Peter, but *to* Peter. Would that all opposition in church was so clean, direct, personal, and honest!

Paul envisions the end of religion, and Christ as "the end of the law."[27] In its place, he pictures the community of faith working through love. The corollary in our conversation is *missio Dei*. Whatever does not come from faith is sin. Your primal identity does not come from your religion. Christ brings a whole new life, the end of religion and the beginning of the church, understood as the community of faith working through love. As such, we

26. Gal 2:11, NRSV.
27. Rom 10:4, NRSV.

arrive at the answer to the question posed by the letter to the Galatians: no religious condition must be met to receive Christ, for in the new creation, the opposition between religious and unreligious no longer exists.

The new creation moves even farther, from religion to economics, to the opposition, the separation, between rich and poor. Money creates both an economic and a social distinction, an unjust one. Money propels the exploitation of the poor by the rich, of slaves by a society of masters. In the Gospels, Jesus speaks repeatedly about money, and in particular about its dangers, about hoarding treasures on earth "where moth and rust consume."[28] Having read the Bible weekly for forty years as I have done, I have heard Jesus: with Zacchaeus in the Sycamore, with Matthew the tax collector, and the widow giving her mite, and the prodigal son squandering, and the man fearful of the talents, and the crafty steward, and rendering to Caesar, and—you see how the list grows?

In new creation, all distinctions, including economic distinction, have gone. There is neither rich nor poor, "neither slave nor free," wrote Paul. He saw what we, still, hardly ever do see: that finally, one's primal identity is not one's place on the map of economic life.

2. Application

It is interesting to remember that John Wesley, at the end of his life, worried about the growing wealth of his poor Methodists. They did what he told them: they earned all they could, they saved all they could, they gave all they could. They prospered—and, in their prosperity, they were endangered. They forgot the poor, once they themselves were no longer poor. Their diligence, frugality, and industry—all wondrously good things—also potentiated the obscurity of their primal identity, and, with it, their primary compassion. No, your primal identity does not come from your wallet. We are not what we spend, nor are we what we

---

28. Matt 6:19, NRSV.

buy. We are stewards, not owners. And, finally, we only truly own that which we give away. One who is accustomed to solving any problem by writing a check is doubly endangered by those grave problems for which no check is large enough.

An old friend, who eventually became a city school superintendent, struggled for thirty-five years to teach the poorest children in our region. I will not sentimentalize his work. The city schools in the northeast are in tough shape. He and I watched our own children hurt by these schools. No, we need not sentimentalize.

But I remember a bright June day, one with a light touch, a little whimsy, and deep wisdom within it. I had left my office for the hospital when I drove past the school that my friend led so well. There on the side lawn, moving in a circle, were four hundred students, fifty teachers and administrators, and a dozen custodians and cooks. There they were—some Black, some white; some rich, some poor; some male, some female; some straight and some gay; Protestant, Catholic, Muslim, Jew; some Republicans, some Democrats; some past puberty, and some a long way from it; some *A* students, and some left behind by systemic failures. But in that hour, they danced together, with a good leader. In that moment, they swayed back and forth to some new Polynesian beat and rhythm. I pulled to the curb to watch, and to pray. It wasn't quite heaven, but you could see it from there: a vision of the new creation in Christ, of diverse primal identities connected as equals, without distinction. *Neither slave nor free.*

Galatians 3:28 points to a clue to another of our great arguments, one which has already caused great harm and which, in our time, threatens an even greater divide. In direct contradiction to the unfortunate 2017 "Nashville Statement,"[29] Paul writes that in Christ, "there is no male and female." In the new creation, there is no gender; gender is swallowed up in victory. Your identity is not to be inferred from creation, but from new creation!

---

29. The Nashville Statement was written by a coalition of conservative evangelical leaders to state their beliefs on human sexuality, including opposition to same-sex marriage and fluid gender identity. See: https://www.tennessean.com/story/news/religion/2017/08/30/what-nashville-statement-and-why-people-talking-it/616064001/.

"NO MALE AND FEMALE": RUMINATIONS ON THE NEW CREATION

This apocalyptic baptismal formula declares the erasure—who says there is nothing radical about Christ?—of the distinction we so heighten, that between male and female.

I know what Paul writes in the Letter to the Romans.[30] He writes of God's creation, and his conclusions, including the true sexual identity of humans as male and female, are based on such. You must ask yourself: which is the crucial Pauline passage, Galatians 3 or Romans 1? The question is a serious one. It is in Galatians that Paul speaks of the new creation which has, by its very existence, transcended creation. There is our identity: not what is natural but what is heavenly about us forms our primary identity.

The trajectory of Paul's preaching in Galatians, and thus in total, makes ample space in our churches for gay people. Your identity does not come from your sexuality, your gender, your orientation. No male and female means no gay and straight, no homosexual and heterosexual. God is doing something new, which includes all in the community of faith working through love, and includes with full grace the full humanity of gay people.

In this respect, let us consider *missio Dei*. God is calling into existence a new community of faith working through love. That is: the Bible itself, from the vantage point of this great mountain passage, opens the way for an understanding of identity that is not just nature or creation, but new creation. This is the community of faith working through love. Here is a place where God is doing something new, revealing something new. And, most strangely, it may be those who are not so easily confined by the creational categories of male and female—those, say, who are both or neither—who are on the edge of the new creation.

We have yet, I doubt, to take seriously the Good News of liberation found in these passages. If you love Jesus, and especially if you love the Bible, then you may find courage to not only defend a moral life in a post-moral culture, but also to preserve freedom for those who have found a whole new life and so become harbingers of a wholly new creation.

---

30. See Rom 1:18–32.

III. Theological Traditions

As we in The United Methodist Church consider the divine mission, we should, perhaps, consider the sources of authority that sustain our interpretation of that mission. I am grateful for the open, broad-minded traditions, especially theological traditions—the spiritual waters in which we learned to swim, from prone float to butterfly—and I am especially grateful for the Wesley quadrilateral, that four-verse hymn to Jesus as our beacon, not our boundary. Its four-sided frame illustrates how, at our best, our love of Christ shapes our love of Scripture and tradition and reason and experience. We are lovers, and knowers too. Yet we are ever in peril, to paraphrase Augustine,[31] of loving what we should use and using what we should love.

There are indeed theological temptations in an unbalanced love of Scripture, tradition, reason, and experience. Let us face them down. Let us face them down together. Let us do so by lifting our voices to admit errancy, affirm equality, explore evolution, and admire experience.

1. Errancy

Your love for Christ shapes your love of Scripture. You love the Bible. You love its Psalmic depths. Psalm 130 comes to my mind. You love its stories and their strange names. Obededom comes to mind. You love its proverbial wisdom. "One person sharpens the wits of another"[32] comes to mind. You love its freedom, its account of the career of freedom. The exodus comes to mind. You love its memory of Jesus. His holding children comes to mind. You love its honesty about religious life. Galatians comes to mind. You love its strangeness. John comes to mind. You love the Bible like Rudolph Bultmann loved it—enough to know it through and through.

You rely on the Holy Scripture to learn to speak of faith, and as the medium of truth for the practice of faith. Around our

---

31. See Augustine, *On Christian Doctrine,* Book I.
32. Prov 27:17, NRSV.

common table today we share this reliance and this love. We all love the Bible. I myself have been studying and teaching the Bible for four decades. The fascinating multiplicity of hearings, here, and the interplay of perspectives present, absent, near, far, known, unknown, religious and unreligious, have a common ground in regard for the Scripture. We may all affirm Mr. Wesley's motto: *homo unius libri*, to be a person of one book.[33]

But the Bible is errant. Matthew recorded the ministry of Jesus decades after it happened (how clear are your own memories from half a century ago?). Luke may not have had all his geographical details straight. John includes the woman caught in adultery, but not in its earliest manuscripts; actually she, poor woman, is in some texts found at the end of Luke. Paul did not write many of the letters attributed to him. The references to slavery in the New Testament are as errant and time bound as is the imperative for female silence in church. The imperative for female silence in church is as errant and time bound as are the references to homosexuality. The references to homosexuality are as errant and time bound as are the several lists of the twelve disciples. Did you ever try to get the list just right? Peter, Andrew, James, and John—and after that it is disputed. The various twelve listings are as errant and time bound as the variations between John and the Synoptic Gospels.

Our Synoptic passages present an idealized memory of something that may, or may not, have happened in the way accounted, somewhere along the Tiberian shore. Nor were they written with such a demand for certainty. They were formed in the faith of the church to form the faith of the church. They are, as Brueggemann once put it, "stylized memories."[34]

It is tempting for us to go on preaching as if the last 250 years of theological study just did not happen. They did. The findings of modern biblical studies do not necessitate that we should deconstruct the Bible to avoid allowing the Bible to deconstruct us, or that we should study the Bible in order to avoid allowing the Bible to study us. In fact, after demythologizing the Bible as

---

33. Wesley, *Wesley's Standard Sermons*, 32.
34. Brueggemann, "Suffering Produces Hope," para. 12.

Bultmann would have us do, we may need to re-mythologize the Bible, too. It is the confidence born of obedience—not some certainty born of fear—that will open the Bible to us. We need not fear truth, however it may be known.

2. Equality

You love the tradition of the church. You love the wisdom found in our shared heritage of faith: those lessons learned across centuries and nations, preserved in words both spoken and written. We rely on tradition as we grasp about for pathways forward.

John Wesley loved the church's tradition, too: enough to study it, and to know it, and to seek its truth. Yet he termed the central ecclesiastical tradition of his time, that of uninterrupted apostolic succession, a "fable."[35] Likewise, we lovers of the church tradition will not be able to grasp for certainty in it if that grasping dehumanizes others.

Baptism is a variously understood practice as traditional and central as Christianity possesses. It is, in some ways, the very doorway to our traditions. Yet listen to Paul writing about baptism to the Corinthians: in his context, he puts baptism second to preaching. For Paul, gospel ever trumps tradition.

We cannot separate tradition from Scripture. Each informs, and builds on, and illustrates, and illuminates, the other. The Bible tells us that the Sabbath was made for the human being, not the other way around; so we, as did earlier generations, enjoy our traditional day of rest. We in The UMC further recognize that our church tradition—reliant, such as it is, on the primacy but not the exclusivity of the Bible—informs, and builds on, and illustrates, and illuminates other texts and oral histories. Consider Wesley's writings. Consider the writings and speeches and stories passed down and around by our other preachers, scholars, and theologians, both historical and contemporary. Consider the new perspective, the new way of looking at things, that you gained through

---

35. Wesley, Eayrs, and Birrell, *Letters of John Wesley*, 91.

the most recent sermon you heard. Our tradition not only bears witness to such growth but integrates it. Though the words of Scripture remain constant, tradition by its very nature remains open to the ever-evolving human experience.

In other words: our tradition is a *living* heritage, not a stagnant one. Encompassed within it are practices and patterns of thought, belief, and action which may be informed by practices and patterns from various historical periods, but are bound by none. Neither are our practices and patterns limited to the influence of a single text, nor a single author, nor a single field of study. The context of historical sacred tradition bears on our interpretation of the Bible, but so does the context of development, of experiences gained and shared by ourselves and by others, right up to and including the present moment.

It is in this context that we must regard the relationship between church tradition and homosexuality. The linkage of heterosexuality and ministry, however traditional, falls before grace and freedom. We roundly cajole our Roman Catholic brethren for their prerequisite to ordination, that combination of the gifts of celibacy and ministry. *You may love God or a woman, but not both at the same time.* But we, by requiring for ordination the universal combination of the gifts of heterosexuality and ministry, apply the same logic: *You may love God or your partner, but not both at the same time.* The coming generations are not going to stay around for it. It is theologically tempting to shore up by keeping out. But it has no future. Equality will triumph over exclusion, just as gospel ever trumps tradition. It is "coming like the glory of the morning on the wave."[36]

3. Evolution

You love the mind, the reason. You love the prospect of learning. You love the life of the mind. You love the Lord with heart and soul

---

36. *United Methodist Hymnal*, no. 717.

and mind. "A mind is a terrible thing to waste."[37] You love reason in the same way that Charles Darwin, a good Anglican, loved reason. You love its capacity to see things differently.

Of course, reason unfettered can produce hatred and holocaust. Learning for its own sake needs the fetters of virtue and piety. Learning, more than anything else, must finally be rooted in loving. Do you hear the request made in our vibrant Psalm 27? To inquire in the temple. Inquiry! Learning! And such inquiry made in the pattern of the Lord's temple will stand on a loving foundation.

The universe is fourteen billion years old.[38] The earth is 4.5 billion years old. Multi-celled organisms appeared at an unparalleled rate around five hundred forty million years ago in the Cambrian explosion; early land plants sprouted perhaps forty million years later; land animals emerged perhaps thirty million years after that. Dinosaurs appeared two hundred forty-five million years ago (and most had disappeared by sixty-six million years ago). Homo sapiens arose three hundred fifteen thousand years ago. Within the thirty trillion cells of every human being are new mutations. Yes, says Francis Collins, onetime leader of the human genome project, and, strikingly, a person of faith: evolution through natural selection by random mutation is a reasonable hypothesis.[39] Yet thirty-eight percent of Americans reject evolution.[40]

"Unite the pair so long disjoined, knowledge and vital piety," implored Charles Wesley, the musical brother of John, in a hymn written in 1763. "Learning and Holiness combined, and Truth and Love, let all men see."[41] Tempting though it may be to disjoin learning and vital piety, it is not loving to disjoin them. The God of

---

37. A phrase attributed to Arthur Fletcher, onetime head of the United Negro College Fund.

38. Facts in this paragraph attributed to Encyclopedia Britannica Online entries "earth," "Cambrian explosion," "plant," "Ordovician period," "dinosaur," "Homo sapiens."

39. Collins, *Language of God,* passim.

40. Swift, "Belief in Creationist View."

41. Wesley and Wesley, *Collection of Hymns,* 341.

Creation is the very God of Redemption. Learning and vital piety go together. Their disjunction may help us cling, for a while, to a kind of faux certainty. But their conjunction is the confidence born of obedience. And their conjunction waits for us on the shoreline of the new creation, the forecourt of *missio Dei*.

4. Experience

You love the life that we are given, the experience of living each morning and evening in faith. Experience in faith is the heart of your love of Christ, and you love Christ. Like Howard Thurman loved the mystical ranges of experience, you do too. You love experience more than enough to examine your experience, to think about and think through what you have seen and done.

In our time, in our culture, and in our world, we must balance religious experience with existential engagement. In our time, a simple or general appeal to the love of experience is neither appealing nor loving. It is not experience but our very existence which lies under the shadow of global violence.

For example: to have any future worthy of the name, we shall need to foreswear preemptive violence. How such a manner of behavior could, at the advent of the United States' "War on Terror," so stealthily enter our civil discourse is a measure of our longing for false certainties. Discussions, or lack thereof, about preemptive, unilateral, imperial, and reckless violent action threaten our very existence. One thinks of Lincoln, who said: "Whenever [I] hear any one arguing for slavery I feel a strong impulse to see it tried on him personally."[42] Not one of us wants this experience. Not one of us wants to be the victim of preemptive violence. We may argue about the need for response, and even for the need of some kind of anticipatory defense. But preemption? It will occlude existence itself. Our future lies on the narrower path of responsive, communal,

---

42. Lincoln, "Speech," 361.

sacrificial, prudent behavior and requires of us, in Niebuhr's phrase, "a spiritual discipline against resentment."[43]

Scripture, tradition, and reason have each, countless times throughout history, been trotted forth as justification for unjustifiable harm. There are, indeed, theological temptations in an unbalanced love of Scripture, tradition, reason, or experience. Let us face them down. Let us face them down together. Let us do so by lifting our voices to admit errancy, affirm equality, explore evolution, and admire existence. The measure of ministry today—a New Creational *missio Dei*, in the tradition of a responsible Christian openness—is found in our willingness to address errancy, equality, evolution, and existence in our rendering of the meaning of traditions.

IV. Reasoned Debate: Finding Our Way

I am grateful to those women and men who have given their lives in ministry to the superintending leadership of our connection, and especially for their steady willingness to reason together with something of an irenic spirit, even across profound differences. A recent set of examples is found in *Finding Our Way: Love and Law in The United Methodist Church*.[44] With some real courage, several church leaders recently published this book of divergent views regarding Christian faith and homosexuality in United Methodism.

With respect for these writers—several of whom we know personally, and a couple of whom I count as real friends—I want to engage their work in reasoned discourse. With respect, and out of love, I differ with most of what is written in *Finding Our Way*. But the singular heart amidst that difference is the gospel itself. I move in four steps here: summary, overview, review, and discussion.

---

43. Niebuhr, *Moral Man*, 248.
44. Job and Alexander, *Finding Our Way*.

"NO MALE AND FEMALE": RUMINATIONS ON THE NEW CREATION

1. Summary

Following a personal introductory frame from the editors, seven UMC general superintendents offer ten- to twenty-page statements about Methodism and gay people. The book concludes with an editorial call to prayer.

Two writers directly state what they personally think regarding gay people, one in affirmation (Melvin Talbert) and one in denial (John Yambasu). Three offer administrative worries (Gregory Palmer—*the discipline must be upheld*), (J. Michael Lowry—*the center cannot hold*), (Kenneth Carter—*the connection needs support*). Two offer mildly inclusive reflections on recent conference level experiences (Hope Morgan Ward, Rosemarie Wenner).

2. Overview

Palmer. Palmer's distinction to affirm "uphold"[45] more than "enforce" (his assigned theme), in interpretation of the *Book of Discipline* has some merit and more grace, and reflects his own sincere, irenic temperament.

Ward. Ward's mildly inclusive reflection on a recent experience honors the "brave witness"[46] of a lesbian couple who suffered the bigotry of the Mississippi Conference to bear witness to their love for each other.

Talbert. Talbert simply and categorically states that the discriminatory language about gays in our church is wrong and cannot claim allegiance, loyalty, or support. The UMC today provides "liturgical resources for pastors who may choose to use facilities of congregations to bless animals, fowls, inanimate objects, and more. Are not our LGBT sisters and brothers of sacred worth like all God's creatures?"[47] Talbert has said and done the right thing well prior to this collection, and his essay is the truest of the seven.

---

45. Palmer, "Enforce," 10.
46. Ward, "Emend," 31.
47. Talbert, "Disobey," 37.

Carter. Carter rightly affirms that every person is created in God's image, and laments theological incoherence. Carter calculates (perhaps accurately, but there is no documentation) that small progressive jurisdictions (we could read here, "northern" could we not?) have more presence, voice, vote and leadership on boards and agencies than do larger and more moderate (we are meant to read here, "southern," are we not?) jurisdictions.

Lowry. Lowry implores us to keep covenant with one another. Many would respond that the question is not whether to keep covenant, but in and about what to keep covenant. If the gospel of Jesus Christ crucified requires the affirmation of the full humanity of gay people and the full rejection of bigotry against sexual minorities in the name of scriptural authority, then the point of covenant is to mutually commit to that gospel. Covenant on behalf of rules of discipline that deny the gospel is false covenant. As Lowry would concede, a substantial UMC majority in this country now affirms same gender marriage and ordination for gay people.

Yambasu. Yambasu equates homosexuality with promiscuity, sexual slavery, and adultery, describes the Bible as infallible, and places the denigration of gay people on par with the venerable inheritance of the ten commandments.[48] His is the voice, or at least the chosen voice for this volume, of Methodism in Africa. To the extent that his view represents African Methodism, it is a communicative benefit to have his remarkable and disappointing perspective stated in the raw.

Wenner concludes: "I pray and work for a future where we will find ways to embrace our diversity on many issues, including human sexuality, allowing us to think differently. Perhaps we may even be able to live with different answers concerning clergy who live in faithful and loving homosexual partnerships and those who choose to conduct same-gender marriages."[49]

---

48. Yambasu, "Unity," 87.
49. Wenner, "Diversity," 98.

3. Review

One feature of this collection—at least, to my mind and ear—is its lack of sustained theological reflection, biblical interpretation, and homiletical assessment. What does the gospel offer to sexual minorities? Where do the crucial Scriptures (John 14, Galatians 3, Ecclesiastes, Amos 5), or the tradition (Bristol, Appomattox, Seneca Falls), or human reason (diagnostic library, psychological research) and experience (case studies and stories of gay children and adults harmed by religious bigotry) intersect with these chapters? Not with heavy frequency, though granted occasional interjections, more from Talbert and Carter than others.

One major exception is the attention Lowry pays to the Jerusalem Conference, and he is right to do so. Yet he addresses the Conference only as described in Acts 15, not Galatians 2. The neglect of Galatians 2 leads to a reading of the passages that is, to my mind, the opposite of their meaning as based on Martyn's earlier-discussed commentary on Galatians and exposition from many others. To neglect the account in Galatians 2 is to deny the imperative that we should seek thematic unity within the Bible's many diverse books.

Lowry argues that the point of the Jerusalem Conference was order: "The famous debate at the Jerusalem Council in Acts 15 is a debate over order, the doctrinal discipline of the church."[50] Was it? Or was it freedom, the freedom for which Christ sets free, the freedom of inclusion over against the inherited order?

As recorded in Galatians 2, the debate at the Jerusalem Conference is about the gospel: Paul, in choosing to preach the gospel to the "genitally unclean"—men who were not circumcised—led the church to leave behind religious order, textual rigidity, and an inherited holiness code. In so doing, the church decided that gospel trumps tradition, and grace trumps order.

Paul leaves behind tradition for gospel. (Freedom, not order.) The uncircumcised are the recipients of the gospel (then),

---

50. Lowry, "Order," 74.

as are gay people (today). It is the perfect biblical citation for our modern-day debate.

4. Discussion

The first task of an interpreter is to honor and affirm the texts interpreted. Text serves as foundation for complex thought which, when shared and discussed and debated, edifies all of us, together and separately. Interpretation has influence; biblical interpretation may become belief, action, policy, even dogma. It is, therefore, important to ground our interpretations in text—in Scripture, in the gospel, in the theology surrounding it. The lack of such is the difficulty that I encounter with *Finding Our Way*. Does the gospel offer grace, freedom, love, acceptance, pardon, and hope to sexual minorities, or not? Does the gospel disdain silent or spoken bigotry against sexual minorities, or not?

In Christ, as we have learned, "there is neither Jew nor Greek, neither slave nor free, there is no male or female." Neither gay nor straight. Are gay people "people," or not? Five-fifths human, or three-fifths human? (We in this country have a bad habit of finding ways to fractionalize the marginalized.) We baptize, confirm, commune, forgive, and bury gay people—yet we somehow cannot find our way to marry or ordain them? We baptize, confirm, commune, marry, ordain, forgive, and bury those who have undergone surgical abortion, and offer the same to those who oppose abortion. Can we not live "in all things charity"?

It may help all of us to rehearse again some of the basic modes of textual interpretation taught and learned years earlier for use with texts biblical and otherwise. Most passages—including your favorite scriptural passage, parable, story, psalm, or teaching—allow more than one faithful reading. There may, for sure, be incongruent readings, but multiple legitimate ones, too. Simply on a non-literalist hermeneutic, diversity of readings is to be expected.

The Bible is but one example. Our own *Book of Discipline* offers signposts for the practice of our communal faith. Our general superintendents, interpreters of the *Book of Discipline,* affirm the value of the book to be interpreted. Once the General Conference has passed off a version of the *Discipline* for another four years, it falls to the bishops, along with others, to interpret and apply it.

We in The UMC allow latitude regarding issues of life and death, abortion and warfare. We admit that, while all abhor war, some are pacifist and some are not, and all are part of The UMC. Why we cannot allow such latitude regarding love and marriage is a mystery and truly says much about the remains of the mind of the church.

We may contrast the church's handling of gender and sexuality with its handling of abortion. The *Book of Discipline* affirms a moderate pro-choice position regarding abortion. But the *Discipline* does not reserve or deny the sacred gifts of marriage and ordination to individuals based on their agreement with the Church's position. We do not exclude from marriage or ordination those who practice surgical abortion, nor those who have had abortions, nor those who have provided pastoral help to others during the course of such a procedure. Neither do we exclude those who reject abortion, those who refuse to practice or affirm others to practice it. We have a position as a church, but we allow for differences in practice—differences that both agree with and conflict with our stated position. We have already found this way to live together in the complexities of faith and humanity. We should now apply this way of living to our position on homosexuality, including the marriage and ordination of gay people.

Note again, based on such latitude as described above, the diversity of reading possible in the *Discipline* itself. So, the dozen affirmations in the discipline of the requirement of pastoral care for gay people may rightly be read as a requirement for pastoral ministry for gay people who are getting married or discerning vocations. Recognition for gay marriage and ordination may be understood as not only permissible, but required of The UMC, to the fulfillment of these paragraphs.

The *Book of Discipline* describes the duties of the pastor surrounding marriage:

> To perform the marriage ceremony after due counsel with the parties involved and in accordance with the laws of the state and the rules of The United Methodist Church. The decision to perform the ceremony shall be the right and responsibility of the pastor.[51]

There is no shading here, no hem or haw. The pastor decides—after due counsel (pastoral care), and in accordance with state law and church rules—whether to marry a couple. No comment is here offered to the situation when state law and church rules, both of which are to be upheld, are different: rightly, the *Discipline* leaves these difficult (pastoral) decisions in the hands of the minister.

So—do we mean this? Will we, as Br. Palmer says, "enforce," or "uphold," the discipline? The *Book of Discipline* places the burden of responsibility clearly and unequivocally upon the pastor, whose "right and responsibility" it is to decide to marry a couple. "The decision to perform the ceremony shall be the right and responsibility of the pastor." Not the General Conference; not the General Superintendent; not the District Superintendent; not the Charge Conference. The pastor. As it should be.

---

51. *Book of Discipline*, ¶340.2.a.3.a.

3

Mark

WE TURN NOW TO the Synoptic Gospels, beginning with Mark, the earliest. To interpret Mark, one needs to develop, over time, a sense of the whole of the Gospel: a sense of the biblical, the liberal biblical theology at work in the full text. We will practice such development by embarking together on a conceptual exercise.

Before you work high, you have to figure out how to get yourself up there. Perhaps you have seen a scaffold surrounding a church steeple under repair, or perhaps you have seen a steeplejack making repairs while hanging many feet off the ground. Steeplejacks do not use scaffolds when making repairs; they use rope and pulleys to hoist themselves up, and they earn, rightly, many hundreds of dollars an hour. As one said to me, quoting Scripture, and speaking of the dangers of height, "Jesus said, 'Lo(w), I am with you.'" Meaning, he continued, "Up high, you are on your own."

The exercise in this chapter imagines a scaffold as the platform, the framework, on which we stand to build or repair the steeples of our faith. Climbing a scaffold affects what we can— and cannot—see and hear and touch, both in the world around us, and in a less physical sense over the course of our spiritual lives. Scaffolds are fundamental, necessary, and crucial. Our responsibility lies in their manner of construction. Are our scaffolds stable? Do they help us, or do they limit us?

Though biblical theology analyzes discreet verses or paragraphs in Scripture, the movement of thought and interpretation is more from the outside in than from the inside out. Each verse requires a unity of perspective for interpretation to proceed. Every verse is embedded in a pericope, and each such passage in a chapter, and each chapter in a book, and each book in the canon itself. Yet each verse ushers in, gives way to, pericope and chapter and book and canon. The scaffolding runs both ways.

By way of such an approach, we exercise our apperception of liberal biblical theology in Mark. We build, together, a scaffold on which to stand, see, hear, build, and repair. We examine our awareness of, assessment of, and allegiance to our scaffolds. In teaching, and more so in preaching, the distillation of the sense and essence of a verse can thereby stand the test of time, and the test of meaning, belonging, and empowerment.

I. Foundation for Ascent

The first five churches in which Jan and I served hired steeplejacks for the minor tiling, shingling, painting, and other repairs needed to maintain small church steeples on small-steepled churches. One was squat enough (the church, I mean, not the jack) that the jack could go up by ladder. Our sixth church (and the seventh, too) was a "tall steeple church." Whenever repairs were needed, the trustees first tried to get by with a steeplejack, to avoid the cost of scaffolding; but most times, no, they needed to spend more. They needed scaffolding. One year, a two-hundred-pound section of copper plate fell off that church's tall steeple onto a University neighborhood street. No one was hurt. Exposure, liability, act of God, randomness—these words appeared in sermons later that month. Scaffolding went up the next week and stayed up for several expensive days.

The interior space of churches also requires endless attention. As with care of the human body after the age of forty, the motto for sanctuary care must be "maintenance, maintenance, maintenance." Owing to the lofty ceilings, maintenance in a sanctuary often requires scaffolding; this comes at a price, which we may try to avoid. Sure, one may prefer to change light bulbs and paint ceilings with a huge ladder and a fearless accomplice. Sure. But the higher the nave—well, I refer you to the adage above: *Lo(w), I am with you*. Low, not high.

Even before any paint is spilled, and even before any long-lasting bulbs are replaced, there is work, there is cost, in a meaningful preparation. So it is, you know, in preaching. The preacher, the interpreter, might swing in the breeze like a steeplejack if the matters of historical interpretation are low fences, but if the height is greater, scaffolding is needed. Major projects require the investment, the firm foundation, of scaffolding. What you see when the work is done is the steeple repaired, the roof replaced, the paint (both coats) applied, the bulbs changed. But before the work is finished, the scaffolding had to be erected so that the work could be done.

When you preach, you may interpret the Gospel flat, in a synchronic—not a diachronic—way. In this way, you may simply read it and make comments on it as you please, assuming the text to be a univocal depiction of purported events or doctrines, and giving little or no thought to the complexities of historical interpretation. In the same way, you may paint the walls of your church by opening the can, stirring the paint, and letting fly. It is a primitive procedure, but you are free to use it. You may fix a roof by hurling shingles to the heavens and hoping that some will land on the roof, to be affixed by nails lobbed up in the same way. You may aim your arm at various fixtures and pitch lightbulbs upward in the hope that some may land in place and, perhaps by way of a little breeze, screw themselves in. There are many examples of this kind of preaching, without scaffolding. Working relatively low on the wall, you might not notice the shortcomings of this method, but I recommend it for neither hearer nor speaker. You would know, were somebody to douse you with a bucket of paint from above; you would know what it would feel like, and how to judge it.

II. Markan Scaffolds

The Gospel of Mark requires scaffolding. We cannot begin to paint until we have someplace to stand. No light bulbs will be changed until we can reach the fixtures. We cannot accomplish the work of preaching until we have found a way to firmly ascend toward the heights of the Gospel's rich complexity. Help me build the scaffolding for our exploration.

The Gospel of Mark is widely considered to be the oldest of the Gospels, likely written between 69 and 73 CE. Mark's composition, editing, comparisons, juxtaposition of sayings, style, and Christology all point to Mark as the earliest gospel.[1] His church may have been in or around Rome, or, more probably, somewhere in Syria.

Although we know Mark's name, we do not know who "Mark" truly was. While his writing purports to recount events that occurred forty years earlier during the ministry of Jesus, its main thrust is toward its own contemporaneous hearers and readers. Mark writes to support and encourage his community, a community of people who had already been embraced by faith. So, it is not an evangelistic tract, and it is not a diary, and it is, emphatically, not a history.

Mark is not great literature. It is not Plato, not Cicero, not Homer. Nor is the Greek of this Gospel a finely tuned instrument; the language used is harsh, coarse, and common. Mark writes neither a timeless philosophical tract nor an ethereal piece of poetry. His is, rather, a "message on target,"[2] a message for the times. It was a message formed in, and for, the life of the author's community.

You will want to know what we can say, then, about Mark's community. If the community was the birthplace of, and primary focus of, and intended audience for the Gospel, you would like to know something about that community. Mark's fellow Christian congregants, we can surmise, are in the main of Gentile,

---

1. Marcus, *Mark 1–8*, 17–56.
2. Marcus, *Mark 1–8*, 37.

not Jewish, birth. He is writing to a particular community of Christians, though the name and location of the community are unknown—only a couple members of his church, Alexander and Rufus, are mentioned by name.[3]

We can glean that the community is persecuted, or is dreading persecution, or both. *Jesus suffered and so do—or so will—you,* is what Mark says. This Gospel prepares its hearers for persecution.

I have used the word "gospel." You have heard the word many times, and you know that it means "good news." It is an old term. You could compare it to "ghost." Gospel is to good news as ghost is to spirit, you might say. Yet Mark names his writing a "gospel." He creates something new.

Mark is a writing unlike any other that preceded it. Today, it is no longer popular, no longer fashionable, to say this,[4] but it is true. Mark's Gospel fits into none of the genres we know from ancient literature. It is not a history, not a biography, not a novel, not an apocalypse, not an essay, not a treatise, not an epistle. Examples of all these were to hand for him. Mark might have written one of any one of them. He did not. He wrote something else and so, in form, in genre, gave us something new: a gospel. His was the first, but not the last.

The Gospel's passages and messages, formed in the life of Mark's community, are announced as memories meant to offer hope. The Gospel's accounts of Jesus's healing and preaching and teaching, all the way to the cross and beyond, were originally offered to a very human group of humans who were trying to make their way along His way. Mark's Gospel is a record of the

---

3. Mark 15:21, NRSV.

4. Marcus, *Mark 1–8,* 65. "Bultmann, indeed, thought that the Gospel genre was a Christian invention and absolutely unprecedented. . . . Partly because of the enormous stature of Bultmann, the Bultmann/Schmidt position on the nonbiographical nature of the Gospels held the field until well into the post–World War II period. But it has gradually been eroded in recent years, on the one hand, by the demonstration that some Hellenistic biographies are more popular than Bultmann and Schmidt gave them credit for being, and, on the other hand, by the argument of redaction and literary critics that the Gospels are more sophisticated than had previously been thought."

preaching of the gospel, the good news of the Christian message, as Mark and his community both received and shaped it. To miss this, or to mistake this, is to miss the main point of both the Gospel and the gospel.

It is in the preaching, in the telling of it, that the gospel arrives, enters, feasts, embraces, loves, and leaves. It is through preaching that one hears a message that makes life meaningful, makes life loving, makes life real. It is by preaching that the Gospel of Mark came to be, as a community over time heard and reheard it, told and retold it, remembered and rehearsed it. Mark preaches the story of Jesus crucified (his past) and risen (his presence). We should not expect narrative linearity, historical accuracy, or recollective precision here.

Most of the New Testament documents are, in one way or another, attempts to preach upon the nature and meaning of baptism. Well, Mark fits that description. What does it mean, here and now, to be a Christian?

III. Upper Planks: A Tale of Two Marks

With a few exceptions, the general shape, heft, and contours of the scaffolding needed to ascend Mark's Gospel, described above, are a matter of broad scholarly consensus. But we have one more tier to erect before we reach our intended position. At this height, the weight of the matter makes the scaffold lean and swing a little; just which planks need to go where, exactly, is uncertain. Here, just at the very top of our reading and hearing of the Gospel of Mark, we need to step carefully.

I put it this way: *ours is a tale of two Marks*. There are two possible ways to interpret Mark's perspectives upon certain aspects of the Christian faith, tradition, and leadership, as experienced by community. Is Mark a moderate critic or is Mark a critical moderate? How you answer will both depend on and indicate your own position on the scaffold.

Moderate critic, critical moderate? That is: does Mark, across the length of his Gospel, actively oppose, and even condemn, others? Or is he carefully moderating—coaching, if you will—the approaches of others? Notwithstanding those characters and viewpoints within the Gospel story clearly meant as critique, is the tone of its criticism polemic, or irenic?

Mark is clearly an apocalyptic writing, although clarity about this has only fully emerged in the last generation or so. Mark expects the end of all things in his own time, and the Markan Jesus instructs his followers accordingly. In fact, Mark expects the culmination of all things, soon and very soon. In this regard, and in regard to his understanding of the cross, Mark has some congruence with the letters of Paul.

Given this apocalyptic perspective, is Mark a critic or a coach?

1. Moderate Critic

The first interpretation—Mark as moderate critic—was most piercingly presented almost forty years ago. First let me give you the outline of the planking in this part of the scaffold, and then let me tell you about the carpenter.

This view presents Mark in combat with the community's failure to remember Jesus's suffering and crucifixion long after the events at Calvary and Golgotha. Strong, spirited evangelists singing only a happy song have caused members of Mark's community to forget their baptism, or its meaning. They expect ease, spiritedness, joy, and soon, a conquering victory over all that plagues and persecutes them. This phenomenon did not originate in Mark's day; rather, the Gospel writer and his community could have traced it back to the mistaken viewpoints of many of the original disciples, including, chiefly, Peter himself. But to all such spiritual triumphalism, Mark says no: he rejects their stance, remembering instead—in delicate detail, based on a source document he has inherited—the story of Jesus's passion.

Mark stays within the fold of stories that he and his community have inherited about Jesus: stories of his teaching and passion, of Galilee and Jerusalem. But Mark tells these stories, in part, with the intention of refuting and criticizing people within the church who had disregarded the reality of earthly suffering, from which the gospel does not deliver any more than Jesus had been delivered from the cross. Saved, yes; delivered, no. According to this interpretation, the heart of Mark's writing conveys a bitter and serious dispute in earliest Christianity about what constitutes discipleship and baptism, and Mark is out to prove his opponents wrong.[5]

Mark's rebuttal of spiritual triumphalism points to Peter's ignorance in the way of the cross and his cowardly denial of Christ in Jerusalem. Mark centers the cross as the denouement of Jesus's purpose and ministry, and he chastises—even condemns—those such as Peter, who would deny it. The titles Mark employs for Jesus are intended to highlight his humanity and, thus, his vulnerability to suffering—a divergence from the "divine man" theologies touted by Mark's opponents. In contrast with Christian teachers who preached nothing but divine power and blessing, Mark downplays the miracles of Jesus, letting them wind away to nothing as the narrative moves inexorably toward the cross, progressively slowing down and focusing the hearers' attention.

Mark draws parallels between the false teachers of his own day and Jesus's misguided disciples, whom he portrays as diabolical dunces, ever failing to grasp the meaning of the message that Jesus emphatically declared to them over and again—"that the Son of Man must undergo great suffering, and be rejected... and be killed."[6] "Mark decides to dramatize the Christological dispute raging between himself and his opponents through the interrelation of Jesus with his disciples during the course of public ministry. That is, he stages the christological debate of his community in a 'historical' drama in which Jesus serves as a surrogate for Mark and the disciples serve as surrogates for Mark's opponents."[7] And, at the end of Mark's Gospel, these false teachers and disciples receive no redemption. *They didn't understand and neither do you,* he seems to say.

---

5. cf. Marcus, *Mark 1–8*, 76–78.
6. Mark 8:31, NRSV.
7. Weeden, *Mark*, 162–3.

The stories of post-resurrection reconciliations between Christ and the disciples, mainly Peter, that are found in the other three Gospels have accustomed us to the assumption that redemption was part of their story. But Mark, we must recall, was the earliest Gospel. When Mark was written, these other books did not yet exist. The others were written later, and they borrowed from Mark, and in some cases seem to have altered what they borrowed to soften or eliminate Mark's polemic bent. And Mark alone leaves the disciples in their folly at the end of the story. Mark is moderate in his criticism, to be sure—though his warnings are dire, he does not harangue, castigate, or overly condemn—but he is a critic at the last.

I am pleased, and honored, to tell you that the person who most powerfully presented this view is a dear friend of mine. Ted Weeden is his name, and he was, in fact, my immediate predecessor in our Rochester church, Asbury First UMC—my eleven years in that pulpit immediately followed his seventeen. He is a Methodist minister who did his doctoral work at Claremont. After several decades, the force and power of his argument stands up and stands out in comparison to the work of others. As with the alternative, there is plenty of evidence to support this sort of scaffold.

2. Critical Moderate

The second interpretation, Mark the critical moderate, has been present for a longer time and, one would say, is still the more dominant position. I have read through the culminating presentation of this position in a two volume Anchor Bible Commentary. (Opening the books, I was interested to find that their author, Joel Marcus, once taught on the faculty of Boston University's School of Theology.)

This Mark does not face strong spirit people committed to an idea of the "divine man," and his community is not so much at daggers drawn; there are differences to be sure, but the disagreements are differences among friends. This Mark is not so negative about miracles. The disciples are mistaken but not malevolent. The titles for Jesus are not so telling of a background conflict. The real trouble comes, primarily, not from within the fold (perish the thought) but from potential deceivers outside of the church. Hence, on this scaffold, Mark has the job of more gently reminding his hearers of the cross, of suffering, of discipline, of the cruciform character of Christianity, in which they believe. He is a moderate—a critical moderate, but a moderate more than a critic.

It can be hard to recognize that our faith tradition may have been born out of serious conflict. It is like family stories: we really don't like to imagine that our family tree is littered with broken branches, dead limbs, crooked roots, and Dutch elm disease. We prefer the vision of the palm tree, majestic and free. So it is with the family tree of our faith. The second option is a more pleasing view; it appeals to our sense of pride in our Christian heritage. But over time, in exploring the Gospel of Mark, I have found Weeden's Mark to be the stronger scaffold, and what we need from a scaffold is not presentation but sturdiness and reliability—not beauty, but strength.

Here is where my feet come down: Marcus appeals to my heart, what I wish were true or truer. But my mind trusts Weeden.

IV. Exploring the Markan Gospel

Mark: moderate or critic? Our passage for exploration is Mark 12:38–44. It is an example of the diversity of reading, of interpretation, offered by biblical text. This passage begins with an attack upon the scribes of old, and so upon the leaders of Mark's church:

> As he taught, he said, "Beware of the scribes, who like to walk around in long robes, and to be greeted with respect in the marketplaces, and to have the best seats in the synagogues and places of honor at banquets! They devour widows' houses and for the sake of appearance say long prayers. They will receive the greater condemnation."[8]

---

8. Mark 12:38–40, NRSV.

The passage teems with criticism, with condemnation. There is venom; there is hurt, too. There is an outsider looking in. *You, too, were outsiders*, the passage recalls. You follow one who sat outside, who resented the robes, the prayers, the stoles, the seats, the feasts, the forgetful unsympathy which occludes human vision and corrupts human life. Be careful: in God's time, the first become last.

The next passage concludes the Gospel's narrative before the passion. Mark paints a portrait of a poor widow, righteous but overshadowed, who has given all she has, her whole life. When it comes to giving, the question is not "how much" but rather "out of how much."

> He sat down opposite the treasury, and watched the crowd putting money into the treasury. Many rich people put in large sums. A poor widow came and put in two small copper coins, which are worth a penny. Then he called his disciples and said to them, "Truly I tell you, this poor widow has put in more than all those who are contributing to the treasury. For all of them have contributed out of their abundance; but she out of her poverty has put in everything she had, all she had to live on."[9]

The disciples summoned by Jesus represent Mark's church, the very members of his church. Just how hard on them is he? The public setting "could hint that the lesson is particularly important for the members of the Markan community," writes Marcus. "Are there perhaps rich people there as well as poor ones, and are the ostentatiousness of the former and their callousness toward the latter among the spiritual dangers besetting Mark's church home?"[10]

Two possible tones can color our reading of this portrait of unjust distance between rich and poor in the Temple, and so in the community of Mark's church. One moderate, a good stewardship lesson. One critical, a call to change. The latter is the truer, the latter is the gospel. The passage shows us Mark the critic, Mark the

---

9. Mark 12:41–44, NRSV.
10. Marcus, *Mark 8–16*, 861.

prophet. He might have Jesus add, *I saw many in the temple that day . . . and it seems as if I saw some of you there, too.*

V. Climbing Down: Applying the Gospel

Here follow three suggestions regarding our awareness of, assessment of, and allegiance to our scaffoldings—those frames of reference from which we see, hear, build, and repair.

We already have our scaffolds in place. Are you aware of those which you have ascended? They color our perception: We see what we expect, or want, to see; we hear what we are accustomed to hearing. And they color our understanding: "All looks yellow to the jaundiced eye."[11]

Yes, we have our scaffolds. Are they the right ones? Are these, yours, the right ones for your life today? Are you aware of your presentiments, your prejudices, your perspectives? Are you? Can you give an account, for example, of your religious perspective? We are more regularly challenged to account for our political perspective, conservative or liberal, or our economic perspective, libertarian or egalitarian, or our cultural perspective, bohemian or bourgeois.

Today the Markan Jesus sits, outside the temple, and turns a moderate or critical eye upon the horizon, upon the whole, upon what purports to represent the good, true, beautiful, and holy. What is your scaffold made of, when you lean toward the realities of dawn and twilight?

Then let me ask you, now that we have awareness, to assess your religious scaffolding. Does it hold? Here are a couple of tests, ways to jump a bit up and down on the board without yet falling: those universal challenges of death and taxes.

Does your religious scaffold hold when you reach out to fix the steeple in the hour of death? Tom Long, our colleague in Atlanta, once preached an op-ed sermon[12] about our cultural spiritual inability to gracefully approach and accept death. He quoted

---

11. Pope, *Essay on Criticism*, 28.
12. Long, "Chronicle of a Death."

nineteenth-century British politician William Gladstone, who said, "Show me the manner in which a nation cares for its dead, and I will measure with mathematical exactness the tender mercies of its people." Long himself recommends some better scaffolding to support our view of death: "People who have learned how to care tenderly for the bodies of the dead are almost surely people who also know how to show mercy to the bodies of the living."

Does your scaffold hold when you face financial extremity? Has the scaffold the strength to hold you up while you look out for that next job, while you look down at the prospect of debt, while you look up at your hope for measured frugality, while you look in toward the same potential greed Jesus saw in the temple of old? If the scaffold wobbles here, you have some work to do.

Have you assessed your scaffold?

Then, to conclude—given awareness, granted assessment—let me ask you something: where is your lasting allegiance? Whose are you? "Where your treasure is, there will your heart be also."[13] Where is your allegiance?

Is it time to change? Is it time to find a better scaffold—I mean perspective—I mean scaffold—I mean worldview—I mean scaffold—I mean faith?

One of our friends sent me this comment on a sermon I once delivered: "I'd further suggest it is time to unleash a more aggressive message: that only stupid people think they are so smart that they can figure out everything for themselves and that if they (and everyone else) just maximize their self-interest we will end up with the best of all possible worlds. Rather, really smart people know that they are both limited but responsible and that their best hope is to join in the company of other faithful people in a life of prayer and study and worship to help illumine the path."

Have you come to a moment of change?

---

13. Matt 6:21, KJV.

VI. Afterward

A long time ago, a preacher and scholar summed up his own way of thinking: "Is thy heart right, as my heart is with thine? I ask no farther question. If it be, give me thy hand."[14]

Can you hear the trust held, affirmed, offered there? *If thy heart be as mine, give me thy hand.* Can you hear the openness, the maturely naïve confidence, the fresh breeze there? *If thy heart be as mine, give me thy hand.* Can you hear the freedom and grace there? It begs to be heard. In its hearing are your health, safety, healing, salvation.

---

14. Wesley, *Character of a Methodist*, 17.

4

Luke

OUR PRACTICE OF THE partnership in the Gospel embraces a generous review of biblical theology in and within the Synoptic traditions. In that spirit, we turn now from the oldest Gospel to the Third, from Mark to Luke. Our exercise here will lead toward the construal and personal appropriation of a liberal biblical theology by means of appreciating the biblical interpretation of the early church.

One of the greatest weaknesses for most of us in ministry, and especially in preaching, is our inattention to the ways in which Scripture would have been interpreted by its first generations of interpreters. Especially, it may be, in Protestant circles, the temptation can be strong to jump immediately from Paul to Luther on Paul, or from John to Wesley on John. So much breadth is lost, then, along the way.

This chapter, as did the previous chapter, exercises such disciplined, ongoing, and very significant work. Let' us explore the liberal biblical theology Luke offers for the church by shifting our perspective, our angle of vision, to see the Lukan horizon. We view the Gospel within the context of its world, and we view the Gospel's world as formed within the context of its community's heritage and traditions. We reflect upon Luke's possible source materials and begin to perceive the depth which stands to be gained by a new awareness, a new examination of the ways in which Luke and his community interpreted the stories and traditions they had inherited.

I. The Lukan Horizon

At the Prado, Spain's wonderful museum now more than two hundred years old, you can stand mesmerized before the paintings of El Greco. "The Adoration of the Shepherds," from 1612, is El Greco's majestic depiction of Jesus' birth according to St. Luke. Barefoot shepherds, their bodies posed in awe and wonder, crowd around the infant and his attendant mother. The Christ Child is bathed in brilliant light that reflects from the countenances of the shepherds.

The story secured in the pages of Luke's Gospel renders Jesus not—as John would have it—here with God before all time began. It renders Jesus not—as Matthew would have it—here among the wise and powerful, the Magi. It renders Jesus here among the poor, among the shepherds. God born among the poor.

What meets you in St. Luke?

By most estimates, the Gospel of Luke was written around the year 90 CE, nearly a generation later than Mark. Its author—who also authored its sequel, the Acts of the Apostles—is unknown to us. We traditionally know him only as Luke the physician, and we come to know him only through the writing itself.

Luke brings us a mixture of materials and makes his own particular use of them. Luke, as did Matthew, knew and repeated most of the earlier Gospel of Mark. But Luke's version reflects changes made along the way—such as in the story of Jesus' rejection by his own hometown (Luke 4)—or places different emphases on the narrative's events.

Luke drew also from a written collection of teachings, now lost, which modern scholars call "Q," from the German *Quelle*, meaning "source."[1] Both Matthew and Luke used this source, combining teachings from Q with other materials to form their unique Gospels. For example, though Luke and Matthew each drew our Lord's Prayer from Q, Luke's version differs slightly from Matthew's, as does his version of the Beatitudes and other teachings that comprise Luke's "Sermon on the Plain" and Matthew's "Sermon on the Mount."

Luke's Gospel includes his own unique source material and original writings, as well. Between Luke 8 and Luke 18, or thereabouts, are long chapters of material not found in Mark, or elsewhere. We have Luke to thank for passing down to us some of our favorite parables, like the Good Samaritan, the Lost Sheep, the Prodigal Son, and the Dishonest Steward.

We have noted some differences between Luke's version of events and the versions in the other Gospels. We have noticed some ways that Luke has construed his Gospel differently than the other writers. How should we conceive of these differences? How did Luke choose to include the material he included? Or, put more simply: what messages does Luke have for us, the hearers, and how does he convey them? These questions will take some time to unravel. We shall do so one step at a time, or one narrative at a time.

There are some outstanding features of the Lukan horizon, which we may simply name as we set forth.

First, *Luke displays a commitment to history*, and an "orderly" one, at that.[2] His narrative organization shows the ways in which the meaning of the gospel can be found in the ordering of historical events. Luke and its sequel, Acts, cast sacred history in a distinctive three-part schema: Israel, Jesus, and Church.[3] The time of Israel concludes with John the Baptist; the time of Jesus concludes with the ascension; the time of the church concludes with the *parousia*, the coming of the Lord on the clouds of heaven at the end of time.

---

1. Encyclopedia Britannica Online, s.v. "Q."
2. Luke 1:1–4, NRSV.
3. cf. Cullmann, Oscar. *Christ and Time: The Primitive Christian Conception of Time and History*. 3rd ed. Eugene, OR: Wipf & Stock, 2018.

Second, *Luke carries an abiding interest in the church* and its essential place in the unfolding of sacred history. The writings in the Third Gospel and of the Acts to follow caught the spirit of Ephesians: "Through the church the wisdom of God in its rich variety might now be made known to the rulers and authorities."[4]

Third, *Luke employs and deploys his own theology,* or theological perspective, which emphasizes history and the divine purpose found therein. This is especially hopeful for us, in that it is an encouragement for us to take the gospel in hand and interpret it according to our own time, location, understanding, and need.

Fourth, *Luke highlights the humanity and compassion of Jesus* in a remarkable way. The Christ of St. Luke is the Christ of magnificent compassion, embodied in the humility of a birth among shepherds. The poor, the injured, women, strangers, and those in dire need all stand out, in Luke, as the recipients and subjects of Jesus' love, mercy, grace, and compassion. It is to this compassion that we now turn.

1. Compassion: He Has Lifted Up the Lowly

Hold most closely the compassion in Luke. At every turn, there is a return to the least, the last, the lost: those at the dawn of life, those at the twilight of life, those in the shadows of life. Notice the compassion Luke describes throughout, permeating the Gospel beginning, middle, and end:

"He has brought down the powerful from their thrones, and lifted up the lowly; he has filled the hungry with good things, and sent the rich away empty."[5]

"The Spirit of the Lord is upon me, because he has anointed me to bring good news to the poor."[6]

---

4. Eph 3:10, NRSV.
5. Luke 1:52–53, NRSV.
6. Luke 4:18, NRSV.

"Blessed are you who are poor, for yours is the kingdom of God."[7]

"What does it profit them if they gain the whole world, but lose or forfeit themselves?"[8]

"Sell your possessions, and give alms. Make purses for yourselves that do not wear out."[9]

"But when you give a banquet, invite the poor, the crippled, the lame, and the blind . . . you will be repaid at the resurrection of the righteous."[10]

"Zacchaeus stood there and said to the Lord, 'Look, half of my possessions, Lord, I will give to the poor.'"[11]

"All of them have contributed out of their abundance, but she out of her poverty has put in all she had to live on."[12]

2. Tradition of Compassion: The Hebrew Scriptures

Luke, by placing such emphasis on compassion, draws on the wellsprings of his community's inheritance from the Older Testament, the Hebrew Scriptures. The Hebrew Scriptures were largely composed during an era of captivity, during the bondage of the Israelites in Babylon. In those dark days, the community of faith keenly recalled their earliest history of God's love and power and compassion. They remembered the God who brought them up out of the land of slavery to the land of milk and honey. The books of the Law and the Prophets and Wisdom in the Old Testament demonstrate a deep-rooted tradition of compassion, such as in Exodus:

> You shall not oppress a resident alien; you know the heart of an alien, for you were aliens in the land of Egypt. For six years you shall sow your land and gather in its yield;

---

7. Luke 6:20, NRSV.
8. Luke 9:25, NRSV.
9. Luke 12:33, NRSV.
10. Luke 14:13–14, NRSV.
11. Luke 19:8, NRSV.
12. Luke 21:4, NRSV.

but the seventh year you shall let it rest and lie fallow, so that the poor of your people may eat.[13]

Once, we were poor ourselves, this verse reminds us; *therefore, there will be justice in our land for the poor.* We know what it means to be poor, to be oppressed, to be outcast, to be downtrodden. You may discover, by searching your extended family histories and memories, what happened to your people in the Great Depression: we learned something—or were reminded of something—during that time of hardship, as did the Israelites dragged, again in chains, to Babylon. Luke, in his appropriation of the Hebrew Scriptures' theology, writes in earshot of Babylon, in the memory of compassion for those who suffer.

Let us read together the books of the Prophets, the very heart of the Older Testament. In all religious literature, in all human history, there is nothing quite as sobering—as piercingly and stingingly direct, with regard to justice—as these sixteen voices, four the louder and twelve the lesser. Malachi teaches tithing. Isaiah affirms holiness. Hosea preaches love. Micah shouts, "what does the LORD require of you but to do justice, and to love kindness, and to walk humbly with your God?"[14] Together, the prophets consistently rail against human greed, human selfishness, human covetousness, human apathy. The harvest for our theme is so plentiful here—there are so many examples—that it is difficult to select just one.

Perhaps Amos will serve. In the eighth century BCE, a shepherd boy from Tekoa went down to the gates of the big city, Jerusalem, and cried out against it. He pilloried the shallow religion of his day. He assaulted his government's reliance—its naïve overreliance—on weapons of war. He bitterly chastised the amoral, postmoral practices of human sexuality of his day. But he saved his real anger for injustice. The Bible trumpets justice—economic justice, justice for the poor, and for all! If all we had were the poetry of that shepherd boy from Tekoa, Amos would be sufficient:

---

13. Exod 23:9–11, NRSV.
14. Mic 6:8, NRSV.

"I will not revoke the punishment; because they sell the righteous for silver, and the needy for a pair of sandals—they who trample the head of the poor into the dust of the earth, and push the afflicted out of the way."[15]

"Hear this word, you cows of Bashan . . . who oppress the poor, who crush the needy, who say to their husbands, 'Bring something to drink!' The Lord GOD has sworn by his holiness: the time is surely coming upon you, when they shall take you away with hooks, even the last of you with fishhooks."[16]

"I hate, I despise your festivals, and I take no delight in your solemn assemblies. . . . Take away from me the noise of your songs; I will not listen to the melody of your harps. But let justice roll down like waters, and righteousness like an ever-flowing stream."[17]

Remember Martin Luther King Jr. reciting this last verse, and others, in the sweltering little jail house of Birmingham, Alabama. His impassioned letter joined scripture, tradition, reason, and experience in its cry for justice, for biblical compassion. "Injustice anywhere is a threat to justice everywhere."[18]

Let us read together the books of Wisdom. Love is for the wise, and justice is the skeleton of love. In the books of Wisdom, we find:

"When the righteous are in authority, the people rejoice; but when the wicked rule, the people groan. . . . The righteous know the rights of the poor; the wicked have no such understanding. . . . If a king judges the poor with equity, his throne will be established forever."[19]

"'Because the poor are despoiled, because the needy groan, I will now rise up,' says the LORD; 'I will place them in the safety for which they long.'"[20]

---

15. Amos 2:6–7, NRSV.
16. Amos 4:1–2, NRSV.
17. Amos 5:21–24, NRSV.
18. King Jr., *Letter from Birmingham City Jail*, 3.
19. Prov 29:2; 29:7; 29:14, NRSV.
20. Ps 12:5, NRSV.

"You would confound the plans of the poor, but the LORD is their refuge."[21]

The most sobering judgment about justice is offered, unexpectedly, by Ecclesiastes. He speaks least directly to the theme, but his philosophy is clear: *I look at all the toil of the sons of men, and I see only vanity.* "What do mortals get from all the toil and strain with which they toil under the sun? For all their days are full of pain, and their work is a vexation; even at night their minds do not rest."[22]

That for which you strive will not last, says Ecclesiastes. *That for which you suffer will not endure.* Over forty years of ministry, I have officiated at eight hundred or so funerals or memorials, each a reminder that justice, not acquisition, endures.

Remember Luke's perspective; remember his interest in history and in the church. Luke writes his Gospel with intention, out of the heritage of compassion, justice, and wisdom passed down in the Hebrew Scriptures. *Do justice, love kindness, and walk humbly with God.*

Remember, also, Luke's stated aim for his Gospel: to order, to organize the narrative in a way that illuminates meaning. Meeting Luke within the context of his world, seeing from his horizon, allows us to gain such depth, perhaps otherwise missed. That is, in Luke 3, John the Baptist, dressed in camel's hair with a diet of locusts and honey (though Luke omits to dress and feed him as Mark so does), is the precursor to Jesus. You cannot get to Christmas without Advent. You cannot come to Bethlehem except by way of the Jordan. You cannot celebrate grace without hearing first the prophetic voice (though we also remember that the prophetic is a part of the gospel, not the heart of the gospel). Every year, the Baptist, out in the dark, cold, miserable, mud-soaked Jordan River, stops us. He stops you. He says the one prayerful word of the precursor, the prophetic word: "Prepare." Then he calls the whole people to prayer: to repentance for

---

21. Ps 14:6, NRSV.
22. Eccl 2:22–23, NRSV.

pervasive sin; to acceptance of pardon as the way out of evil and hurt; to assurance of grace.

Prayer is what comes before the rest, as Sunday morning is meant to come before the rest (of the week). Are we getting off on the right foot, week by week?

John the Baptist would want to know. Look carefully at what Luke says about him. See the Lukan Baptist, different from John the Baptist in Mark. Mark, twenty years before, began his Gospel with the Baptist, "the voice of one crying out in the wilderness."[23]

Not Luke. Twenty years after Mark, Luke wants John put in particular context. In exercise of liberal biblical theology, we want to hear the gospel *in the Gospels*. Luke says something different from what he borrowed from Mark. That should give us confidence, as we preach, to take the gospel in hand and apply it to our own condition, to our own time, as the first gospel writers all did.

So, Luke has a history that precedes the precursor. This history, an orderly one, tells of the conjoint mysterious births of John and Jesus. This history, an orderly one, gives singing voice to Zechariah and Mary. This history, an orderly one, acknowledges the days of Caesar Augustus and Quirinius. This history, an orderly one, honors Joseph and paints, as did El Greco, shepherds in the firelight of the cradle. This history, an orderly one, makes a little space for the childhood of Jesus, in woe and weal both—circumcision, presentation, growth in wisdom, and temple teaching. Only then does Luke allow the Baptist to appear. But even here, the orderly history prevails: fifteen years, Tiberius Caesar, Pontius Pilate, Herod and Philip, unpronounceable regions, eminently forgettable tetrarchs, and priesthoods ("a six-fold synchronism," as Bultmann wryly remarks[24]). Luke is making sure Jesus has his feet firmly planted in history—of both secular Empire and sacred Temple—and an orderly history, at that. So, for us, our engagement with history, under the influence of the Gospel of Luke, matters, counts, lasts, is lastingly real.

---

23. Mark 1:3, NRSV.
24. Bultmann, *History of the Synoptic Tradition*, 362.

II. Authority of Scripture; Pragmatism of Practice

Our New Testament came together in the century that followed the writing of Luke. The books of the New Testament were written between the year AD 50 (1 Thessalonians) and AD 160 (2 Peter). But they were not put together into a single canon until (at earliest record) the year AD 175, as recorded in the Canon Muratori. Their collection and canonization happened in a curious way.

Marcion, the most popular preacher in Rome in AD 150, the son of an eastern ship builder, was a Christian Gnostic who put together the first proto-New Testament. As a Gnostic, Marcion separated the God of creation from the God of redemption. He believed that the God of redemption, the Father of the Lord Jesus Christ, was not the same god who created the material world.

To solidify his position, Marcion put together a canon of sorts, heavily weighted with redemption, which included the Gospel of Luke and the Letters of Paul. Notice all that was missing from his compilation—no Hebrew Scriptures, neither Law nor Prophets nor Writings; no other Gospels, Matthew or Mark or John; no other Letters, Peter or John or Jude. (It would have made teaching the Bible much simpler!)

Well, the emerging church came along and quashed Marcion's compilation, and excommunicated him for good measure. The church reconnected creation and redemption, and added Law, Prophets, and Writings; Matthew, Mark and John; the Letters of Peter, John, and Jude (and let's not forget the Revelation) to make of the Bible not a short collection of ten books but sixty-six books in two testaments. That makes teaching the Bible less simple! But you see, the Bible has a story, too. Luke's account, to Marcion's theological mind and within his time, carried such significance that it deserved a spot in Marcion's slim compilation. In our day, one might think of it this way: the Gospel of Luke played in the pre-season games, but also made it to the Super Bowl!

Our Scripture is holy—is the word of God—because, week by week, we read it and listen to it for the divine word. We stand on the shoulders of the ancients, stretching back two and three thousand years, for whom these words were also holy. They outlast us, these words of holy writ. They uplift us. They reshape us. They return us to our rightful minds.

The authority of Scripture lies in a very pragmatic garden of practice: where else would we possibly want to be, come Sunday, than in earshot of that Word? We do this every week, all the four thousand Sundays of our lives. Scripture acquires authority out of its longtime traditional use. Scripture exudes authority as the mind, our gift of reason, explores the caverns and caves, the stalactites and stalagmites, the dark recesses of venerable words. Scripture, in our own hearing, our own recitation, our own living, our own experience, pierces the heart with authority. Tradition, reason, and experience *crown* Holy Scripture with—authority.

5

Matthew

EVERY GOSPEL TAKES A perspective different from the others. The freedom we have, to interpret the gospel for ourselves, begins with the diversity that exists among the Gospels themselves.

We have so far discussed Mark, the moderate critic or critical moderate, and Luke, "the physician," the historian. Later, we will discuss John, the most different of them all. Now we follow the trail of Jesus' life, death, and destiny in another, different, strange Gospel: the Gospel of Matthew.

Matthew's is the Gospel placed at the beginning of the New Testament, in part because of its popularity in the emerging church. As did Luke, Matthew relied on Mark and on the teaching document called Q to compose his Gospel, and, as did Luke, Matthew integrated some of his own particular material, (including in Matthew 1, which we explore in this chapter). Yet in contrast to Luke, whose primary interest was an "orderly" recounting of history,[1] Matthew divided his Gospel in five parts according to careful pedagogical rendering befitting Matthew's traditional role as teacher:

---

1. Luke 1:3, NRSV.

He first tells of the *birth* of Christ. Then he tells of the *teaching* of Christ. Then he tells of the *healing* of Christ. Then he tells of the *cross* of the Christ. Then cometh the *resurrection* of Christ.

In five moves he is teaching us, Matthew the teacher.

Such an organization moves Matthew away from Luke—moving from the History Department to the Religion Department, you could say. Luke orders the history of the Gospel in order to trace out the meaning of historical events; now we find Matthew organizing the Gospel narratives so as to bring attention to their spiritual significance. In so doing, Matthew brings us into another world, out into another world, out into the midst of another world. We have moved from history to religion, from narrative to doctrine. *Whereas Luke orders meaning according to history, Matthew orders history according to meaning.*

Using two passages as our inroad, we will engage with Matthew's perspective to explore the liberal biblical theology offered by his Gospel. We first discuss Matthew 1, the story of Jesus's birth, which highlights the awesome strangeness of the message and the teachings or doctrine involved . . . and the unique centrality of Christ to the Gospel teaching. We then move to Matthew 24, the promise of "the coming of the Son of Man" and its relevance to our future. Here our exercise takes the form of a historical-critical exploration in the model of a four-part chorus, in which the different voices harmonize and interweave in the experience of the modern listener.

I. Matthew 1: Christmas

Late one night some years ago, snow fell lightly along the St. Lawrence, that river in the far north that traces part of this country's boundary with its northern neighbor. Coming over the border from Canada, and down south from the river, one enters a barren, flat land. In the moonlight, the fallow northern fields lie strange and difficult and stern, the farms all dormant or quiet. The dark moonscape flanking the road—pock-marked with valleys and an occasional farmhouse—lies silent. Past midnight on this winter night, the residents are asleep. They know snow there, on the riverbank. With pelting flakes covering the windshield and darkening the moon, nature makes a seamless shroud, "blacker than a hundred midnights down in a cypress swamp."[2]

To step aside from the world of our own doing puts us out into the dark, into strange and unfamiliar territory, into the realm where angels dwell. To find ourselves outside the world of our control and comfort puts us out into the cold moonlight, the place of the uncanny. A return to church can be such a place. A sudden diagnosis can be such a place. An unplanned revisit to an old anger can be such a place. Aging can be such a place. Unemployment can be such a place. Loss of breath can be such a place. The desire to end something before it is really ended can be such a place. A shooting war—on the ground, not from the technological safety of many thousand feet, but in Syria, say, or Ukraine, say—can be such a place.

This darkness lies beyond the stream that imports information, sustenance, and camaraderie into our homes and lives. It is, for all its unfamiliarity away from the blue haze of the computer screen, a wondrous darkness. Here, the lights of the city, the comfort of urban dwellers, shroud and shadow. To step aside from the world of our own doing puts us out into the dark, the realm of angels.

Here is the Good News of Advent: in this darkness, an angel voice announces Jesus Christ, the grace of Almighty God.

1. An Unfamiliar Story

Let us carefully take an attentive look at the Gospel of Jesus Christ announced in Matthew. Christmas, as a cultural break from the patterns of daily life, provides a seam, an opening, for grace, both apart from religion and as a part of religion. The light of God rests in your hearts; you are given it to illumine your hearts and minds,

---

2. Johnson, "The Creation," 17.

to cultivate peace and hope all through the coming year. May we listen again for the true, the good, the right, the lasting?

"The birth of Jesus happened in this way..."

Which way? How quick we are to speak, to stare, to decide, to judge. To know, or think we know. One teacher said to one student: "Your abundant knowledge stands in the way of your real education." I was glad for the advice. How firm is our ostensible grasp of the ineffable, the wondrous, the real? *Our* reverence, unlike that of the Holy Scripture, too often lacks the discomfort of travel, the fear of the unknown, the quaking before angels, the conception of—let alone by—the Holy Spirit. Look forward in your calendar a few weeks: Kings, shepherds, Joseph and Mary. If we are not careful, the Advent and Christmas seasons, in which we recall the story and the meaning of Jesus's birth, become so familiar, so cozy: a habituated rehearsal into which we ease, lulled by newer habits of casual worship, near and far.

But the series of familiar events is not the story of the Scripture. The Bible tells, by angel voice, a strange and difficult and even stern story. Though this story may help us more than all manner of cozy familiarity, it will only engage us when we realize—at last or at first—that it has never been easy to lead a Christian life. Such a life, as Ernest Tittle constantly repeated, is meant for heroes and heroines.[3] As Thurman said: a crown to grow into.[4]

Matthew 1 tells of the birth of Christ, of Jesus Christ (though a later scribe dropped "Jesus," most texts hold to it). Listen to his *unfamiliar* account: a virgin is with child; a husband, who is not yet a husband, resolves not to take revenge; an angel appears in a dream; the angel, in the dream, interprets the Scripture; the man obeys the angel voice; the man accepts the angel's name for what his betrothed conceives. A virgin birth, a resolute husband, *an angel*

---

3. See, for example: *Foolishness of Preaching*, 241–255, 286–300; *Jesus After Nineteen Centuries*, 173–194.

4. Thurman, *Jesus and the Disinherited*, 96. "This is how Jesus demonstrated reverence for personality. He met the woman where she was, and he treated her as if she were already where she now willed to be.... He placed a crown over her head which for the rest of her life she would keep trying to grow tall enough to wear."

voice, a trusting woman, a name transmitted in a dream—strange, unprecedented territory. We do not live in a world of virgin births, resolute husbands, angel voices, trusting dreamers, or names dropped from on high. We prefer to think our world is, rather, a world of our own determinations, our own creation.

By attention to conscience and compassion, by opposition to indecency and indifference, Matthew intended to order the meaning of the history of the gospel. Matthew's writings show his own perspective, some of which involves a developing and developed Christology, an understanding of Christ, forged as Matthew apparently fought a battle on two fronts: against fundamental conservatives to one side, and against spiritual radicals to the other. In Matthew, gospel continues to trump tradition, as in Paul's Letters; but, as in the Letters to Timothy, tradition itself is a bulwark to defend the gospel. Matthew is trying to guide his part of the early church between the Scylla of the tightly tethered and the Charybdis of the tether-less.

Matthew emphasizes the role of law, of the law, of laws. He is a legalist, whether or not he was Jewish (the general assumption, though some argue otherwise). For Matthew, the birth narrative conveys the proper ordering of the meaning of the history of the Gospel. Birth narratives have meaning (as the rhetoric of several previous presidential campaigns in this country have reminded us). *Where did he come from? Who are his parents? Who are his people? Whose birth do we celebrate, anyway? Who formed him, He who now forms us?*

Some answers are found earlier in the chapter, in the first half of Matthew 1. Before the unfamiliar narratives of Christ's conception and birth are the counting of the generations from Adam to Christ—fourteen by fourteen by fourteen, are the generations—from Abraham to David; David to Babylon; Babylon to Christ.[5] The cord of the messianic line runs from Abraham to Joseph, who was betrothed to Mary. To Joseph. To and through Joseph.

---

5. Matt 1:7, NRSV.

Abraham. Isaac. Jacob. Judah. Tamar. Amminadab. Boaz. Ruth. Jesse. David. Solomon. Uriah. Rehoboam. Jehoshaphat. Amos. Josiah. Jechoniah. Zerubbabel. Zadok. Eleazar. Matthan. Jacob. Joseph.

Every one of these names is worth a sermon! We can learn of Jesus's people, his parents, his ancestors, if we choose to do so. We can understand his heritage and earthly origins.

2. An Unfamiliar Name

A student who read Genesis and Matthew for the first time said, "This is so different from the way we think. No one is that awestruck by God."

Today, as during the 1950s, the fashionable belief in God is a general one. There is a God and God is with us, we believe. The pantheist, the spiritualist, the nationalist, the literalist, and many a Methodist can agree. How easily is such a conviction celebrated? Too easily. God is with us in nature, in the homeland, in the Bible, in the religious organization. God is with us. A tidy tale. God is all and everywhere, with us; Emmanuel in trees, in dreams, in politics, writings, in religion. It is the same. God is everywhere! His name shall be called Emmanuel! This we find familiar and cozy.

But the angel voice says otherwise.

It is fitting that the first sermon, the first interpretation in the Gospel of Matthew, is offered by an angel. What other voice would be fit to herald such news? Yes, an angel: "She will bear a son, and you are to name him Jesus, for he will save his people from their sins."[6] How strange this account appears when carefully studied! The angel's announcement interprets for us the prophet meaning of the words of Isaiah:

> All this took place to fulfill what had been spoken by the Lord through the prophet:
>
> Look, the virgin shall become pregnant and bear a son,

---

6. Matt 1:21, NRSV.

and they shall name him Emmanuel," which means, "God is with us."[7]

His sermon—the angel's sermon, Matthew's sermon—purports to tell us about the meaning of the birth of Christ and therefore—as is the magisterial claim—about the meaning of life. We shall want to bear down quietly, and listen . . . Now Isaiah had said that the child should be called "Emmanuel," or "God with us." God, present. Present. Present. Emmanuel. Come Emmanuel. How could any sermon, any interpretation, even by an angel, fathom the meaning of this?

The angel gives another name, a strange, stern, unfamiliar name. Read, hear, of another name: not just Emmanuel, a name of Advent and Christmas, but a name fit for travel, darkness, and places of fear. It is a name spattered with the blood of history. It is a name that fits in a manger. It is a name that cries out for response. It is a winter name, a name in the dark, a name that sends a fierce, cold wind across the unbroken heart. We feel a chill. It is a name that burns a bright flame for every kind of love. It warms us, now. It is a name that charms fears, opens prisons, brings music of life and health and peace. The Matthean angel gives another name: particular, not universal; a name that means one thing, not everything; a hedgehog name, not a fox name.[8] A name above every name. Whose birth do we celebrate, anyway?

"You are to name him Jesus, for he will save his people from their sins."[9]

Jesus is the name of a person. The angel voice of the Lord gives a sermon, replacing "Emmanuel" with the name Jesus, which, being translated, means "he will save" or "God saves." *God with us*, replaced with *God saves*. Mary bore a son, Jesus, who saves from sin. She did not bring into the world an airy belief in the general proposition that God—somehow, somewhere,

---

7. Matt 1:22–23, NRSV.

8. *The Hedgehog and the Fox* is an essay by philosopher Isaiah Berlin, published as a book in 1953.

9. Matt 1:21, NRSV.

anyhow, anywhere—is with us. This name, Jesus, has personal, profound meaning for you and me.

He whom Isaiah called Emmanuel the Angel further named—or renamed—Jesus. Strange, difficult, stern. It means, bluntly, that God enters your life to free you from your besetting sin. Not in trees, dreams, votes, words, or committees, but in person. "He will save his people from their sins." You will know him—if he be known at all—as he saves you. Christ was born to save.

> To save a globe from the sin of climate exhaust
>
> To save a world from the sin of nuclear holocaust
>
> To save a nation from the sin of pride
>
> To save a generation from the sin of greed
>
> To save a church from the sin of self-congratulation
>
> To save a man from alcohol, a woman from suicide, a boy from drugs, a girl from opioids, a family from disaster
>
> To save his people from their sin
>
> To save souls, to set us on the road to heaven.

Such is the name of Jesus: a name that cries out for response, for a people who can acknowledge and confess their sins, for the necessity of saying *thank you, please, and I'm sorry*. Can we become that kind of people? Can we become people who name God not everything, but one thing: the way to freedom from bondage? Can we become people who share the transforming friendship through which all manner of entrapment dies, the gradually deepening friendship with Jesus Christ, in person, who saves us from our sins? Can this friendship be ours? The Angel Voice commends its path to you.

The wondrous news from the darkness, if you can hear and believe an angel, is not just that God is *with* us, but that truly God is *for* us. The good news is not only that God is with us, but also that God is for us.

II. Matthew 24: A Choral Metaphor

One of the foremost delights of life at Marsh Chapel is its musical soundtrack. One who, disheveled and rain-soaked and late to a meeting, rushes past the open sanctuary door might be greeted, and refreshed, by the many-voiced harmonies of a joyous gospel anthem. One sitting quietly in a back office might unexpectedly be reached by strains tender or furious, regimental or graceful, from the many-piped organ. The grand organ that anchors the front of the nave is the same instrument installed upon the building's completion in 1950, though it has—as we all would have after seventy-some years—weathered some refurbishment. Elaborate carvings in the burnished wood of its screen panels show Saint Cecilia, the patron saint of music, holding a portable organ, and Saint Gregory, the namesake of Gregorian chant, with a dove on his shoulder and a monochord in his hands. This grand display is a fitting reflection of the essentiality of music at Marsh Chapel.

Peering closely at the wooden newel posts flanking the choir stalls, one will see carvings of the heads of composers Georg Friedrich Handel and Johann Sebastian Bach. The works of Bach have been particularly central to our experience. We annually present a series of four Bach cantatas in their original liturgical context, and often perform the *St. John Passion* during Holy Week. Perhaps you have heard these transcendent works. A four-part choir, supported by an orchestra, sings the words of Scripture as Bach set them to music. Each "voice" of the choir contributes something different to the glorious soundscape: the low, low basses keep a steady rhythmic underpinning; the tenors deliver their lyrical message with clarion voice; the altos nurture us in tones rich and full, never strident; and the sopranos soar above it all.

It is perhaps inevitable, with such a musical heritage ringing in the ears, that a four-part choral design would impose itself upon the analysis of Gospel passages. In the same way we drew inspiration from John Wesley's four-sided structure, so shall we draw inspiration from a metaphor that celebrates the diversity of voices singing the truth of Scripture. In metaphor, we might imagine one voice as Jesus; one as the Church; one as Matthew, our narrator; and one as Later Tradition. One should not expect to find literalism here, for these are not the parts "assigned" to these voices in Bach's work. Rather, our exercise toward a liberal biblical theology asks us to observe the insight to be gained by a deconstruction of sorts, understanding the contribution made by each independent voice to the magnificent, musical whole. We apply this metaphorical device to a passage in the twenty-fourth chapter of the Gospel bearing the name of Matthew.

> But about that day and hour no one knows, neither the angels of heaven, nor the Son, but only the Father. For as the days of Noah were, so will be the coming of the Son of Man. For as in those days before the flood they were eating and drinking, marrying and giving in marriage, until the day Noah entered the ark, and they knew nothing until the flood came and swept them all away, so too will be the coming of the Son of Man. Then two will be in the field; one will be taken and one will be left. Two women will be grinding meal together; one will be taken and one will be left. Keep awake therefore, for you do not know on what day your Lord is coming. But understand this: if the owner of the house had known in what part of the night the thief was coming, he would have stayed awake and would not have let his house be broken into. Therefore you also must be ready, for the Son of Man is coming at an unexpected hour.[10]

The gist of Matthew 24 is clear enough: we cannot see or know the future. We ought to live on tiptoe, on the *qui vive*. Health there is, to be sure, and succor, in a full acceptance and recognition of such a humble epistemology and such a rigorous ethic. Let us admit, to the bone, our *cloud of unknowing*[11] about the days and hours to come; let us live every day, and every hour of every day, as if it were our last. Song and sacrament, sermon and Eucharist: they will guide us along this very path, this very day.

---

10. Matt 24:36–44, NRSV.
11. Pseudo-Dionysus, *The Cloud of Unknowing*.

Less clear is what is meant by "the coming of the Son of Man." Who is the person so named, and what did he actually say, here, and what is the nature of his coming? On what score did the primitive Christian community remember and rehearse his teaching? Who is this narrator Matthew, and did he have a horse in this race? How has the church, age to age, interpreted the passage? We find in these questions not a cacophony but our four-part chorus, and we will listen to each voice singly before addressing the question posed by their combined harmony: what difference—existential difference, everlasting difference—does any of this make?

First, Jesus. Jesus may have claimed the phrase "the Son of Man," though many have judged that it is a later church appellation. It may have been both. The phrase, coming out of Daniel chapter 7 and the stock Jewish apocalyptic of Jesus's day, was as much a part of his environment, of his day and age, as the sandals on his feet, the donkey which he rode, the Aramaic which he spoke, the Palestinian countryside which he loved, and the end of time which he expected. Did the historical Jesus understand himself to be that figure? We cannot see and we cannot say, though many scholars will say no—that what, if anything, we can learn about the historical Jesus from passages like this is extremely slight. It is in fact the author of Mark and the author Enoch who have given us the concept of the "Son of Man" in its full sense,[12] and it is Matthew, alone among the Gospel writers, who uses "PAROUSIA as a technical term for the coming of Jesus as Son of man."[13] In Matthew, the voices of the author (narrator), his community (church), and religious-cultural milieu (tradition) sing loudest; the *soprano* voice of Jesus is far lighter than we might expect or prefer. Yet as is so common in sacred music throughout history, the soprano voice—even when only dimly perceivable—may be the voice carrying the melody.

Second, Church. The early church grasped literalism in the apocalyptic language of the Synoptic Gospels. As did Mark and Luke, Matthew carries forward the end-of-the-world predictions

---

12. Perrin, "Son of Man," IDBS, 833–5.
13. Perrin, "Son of Man," IDBS, 836.

he inherited. The Revised Common Lectionary omits the apparently mistaken acclamation of Matthew 24:34, but we should hear it: "Truly I tell you, this generation will not pass away until all these things have taken place."[14] The earlier church, like the waiting family in *The Glass Menagerie*, has hung onto the fragile mementos of a person who—like that telephone operator "who had fallen in love with long distances"[15]—would not return. That generation and seventy others have passed away before any of this has taken place. No longer do we expect—literally expect, immediately expect—these portents. Nor should we. Such predictions are part of the apocalyptic language and imagery which was the mother of the New Testament and, consequently, the mother of all Christian theology since. The Son of Man was the favorite child of that mother, and she has drawn up short, in hope of his return. Yet for those whose lives have stalled in waiting, like those who preserve the menagerie of fine glass, "hope deferred makes the heart sick."[16] A long, low, *alto* aria, this.

Third, Matthew. To his credit and to our benefit, our narrator makes his own editorial moves that accommodate the language he has taken from Mark 13. The point of apocalyptic eschatology, here and in the sibling Synoptic passages, is ethical persuasion. *Watch. Be ready. Live with your teeth set. Let the servants, the leaders of Matthew's day, be found faithful.* After thirty-nine excoriating verses in chapter 23, directed against the Pharisees (say, religious leaders in general)—those hypocrites, "like whitewashed tombs, which on the outside look beautiful, but inside they are full of the bones of the dead and of all kinds of filth"[17]—baring the hard truth about reli-

---

14. Matt 24:34, NRSV.

15. In Tennessee Williams' 1944 play *The Glass Menagerie*, the Wingfield family patriarch is a key figure whose presence permeates the play despite the character's complete absence from it. Readers discover, gradually, the emotional effects of his departure on his family. A recurring witticism portrays Wingfield as a telephone man who prefers long distances, as in: "I married a man who worked for the telephone company! . . . A telephone man who—fell in love with long-distance!"

16. Proverbs 13:12, NRSV.

17. Matt 23:27, NRSV.

gion at its worst—and, after forty-three further verses of end-time language in chapter 24, Matthew's tenor part rings out. He delivers his sermon: *you must be ready; the figure of the future is coming at an hour you do not expect.* Hail the Matthew *tenor.*

Fourth, Tradition. The church scrambled to reinvent and reinterpret. *Basso profundo.* One example, found early in our passage from Matthew, will suffice: "about that day and hour no one knows, neither the angels of heaven, nor the Son, but only the Father."[18] But some Gospel manuscripts leave out "nor the Son,"[19] subtly reinventing and reinterpreting the verse in deference to Jesus' later and higher Person. Except for occasional oddball readings (like the Montanists in the second century and the fundamentalists in the twenty-first), the church's predominant view has always been that the Gospel's apocalyptic language and imagery convey the future as unknowable (*even to the Son!*), and the present as unrepeatable. *The future as unknowable, and the present as unrepeatable.* The future slips past us, already flying down the road into the past, just as soon as we reach out to grasp it. The present itself is no more scrutable, with its portions of past and future tangled permanently together. We do have the past—neither dead nor past. Or do we? Memory and memoir spill into each other with the greatest of ease. The moment is a veritable mystery.

What answer do we find in the combined harmony of our four-part chorus? Jesus, Church, Matthew, Later Tradition—how do we hear these voices together? One searcher believed that music presents an opportunity to encounter God.[20] Many among us share the sense that music, performed, is a close approximation of God, the presence of God, the proof of God. Music is a veritable mystery. "My body" and "My blood": these are veritable mysteries, so-named mystery, *sacramentum,* to this day. One trusted Christian—it may have been you—sensed grace upon grace, unlike any other, in the grace of the Eucharist. How shall we respond?

---

18. Matt 24:36, NRSV.

19. As reflected in various translations, for example: KJ21; BRG; DARBY; DRA; GNV; JUB; KJV; MEV; NET; NKJV; NMB; RGT; WEB; WYC; YLT.

20. See: Augustine, *De Musica.*

Sleepers, awake! There is not an infinite amount of unforeseen future in which to come awake and to become alive! There does come a time when it—allowing for the valence of "it" to be as broad as the ocean and as wide as life—is too late. You do not have forever to invest yourself in deep rivers of Holy Scripture—whatever they may be for you. It takes time to allow the Holy to make you whole. *Begin.*

You do not have forever to seek, in the back roads of some tradition, whatever it may be for you, the corresponding hearts and minds which and who will give you back your own-most self. It takes time to uncover others who have had the same quirky interests and fears you do. *Begin.* Mr. Ed McLure, a longtime member of the Marsh Chapel community, our brother in Christ now passed on, used to say: "Politically correct without spiritual respect—is suspect." *Begin.* You do not have forever to sift and think through what you think about what lasts and matters and counts and works. Careers, jobs, employment, work—seek them out, but know that work alone will neither make you human nor allow you to become a real human being. Life is about vocation and avocation, not merely about employment and unemployment. The world is selling you a bill of goods, if you think that life is about money and employment. Be watchful. It takes time to self-interpret that deceptively crushing verse, "let your light shine before others."[21] *Begin. You also must be ready, for the Son of Man is coming at an unexpected hour.*

"We all hope to have a part in heaven, that world of love of which we have heard,"[22] wrote our near neighbor, Jonathan Edwards, a mere three hundred years ago.

> This is the way to be like the inhabitants of heaven. You have heard how they love one another; and therefore they, and they only, are conformed to them who live in love in this world. . . . And by living in love in this world the saints partake of a like sort of inward peace

---

21. Matt 5:16, NRSV.
22. Edwards, "Heaven Is a World of Love," 271.

and sweetness. It is in this way that you are to have the foretastes of heavenly pleasures and delights.

... A frame of holy love to God and Christ, and a spirit of love and peace to men greatly disposes and fits the heart for a sense of the excellence and sweetness of heavenly objects. It gives a relish of them. It, as it were, opens the windows by which the light of heaven shines in upon the soul....

... By living a life of love, you will be in the way to heaven. As heaven is a world of love, so the way to heaven is the way of love. This will best prepare you for heaven, and make you meet for an inheritance with the saints in that land of light and love. And if ever you arrive at heaven, faith and love must be the wings which must carry you there.[23]

We cannot see or know the future, Matthew 24 reminds us. Let us live every day as if it were our last. How do we do this? *Live in love,* counsels Edwards. When do we start? *Now. Begin.* You do not have forever to experience Presence. It is presence, spirit, good for which we long, for which—nay, for Whom—we are made. It takes time to find authentic habits of being: what makes the heart to sing, the soul to pray, the spirit to preach. Your heart, not someone else's; your soul, not someone else's; your spirit, not someone else's. *Begin.*

You also must be ready, for the Son of Man is coming at an unexpected hour.

---

23. Edwards, "Heaven Is a World of Love," 271–2.

6

John

YOU LOVE ALL THE Gospels. One there is, though, which from antiquity has been known as the sublime, "the spiritual gospel."[1] We shall ascend, today, to the craggy paths and rarified air of the ancient Gospel of St. John the Divine.

The Fourth Gospel is very "different." It is far more different from the Synoptic Gospels we have just engaged, and far more different from the other New Testament books, than its current location and home in the canon would make it seem. As Dodd put it: "The fact is that the Fourth Gospel belongs only in part to the same class with the Synoptics."[2]

We will return often, in this chapter, to this idea of difference, of change. The Fourth Gospel was born from disappointment, from the pain wrought by change, and it illustrates a way forward. Not festering in hurt, not paralyzed by the ache of dislocation and departure, but moving forward in freedom, grace, and love. Set before us by John's community is an invitation—presented by means of example—toward courage, toward the unity of Scripture

---

1. See, for example: Eusebius, "Book Six," 251.
2. Dodd, *Fourth Gospel*, 4.

and tradition with experience in Christ, toward an "embraceable variant."[3] In the midst of struggle, John's community grasped for the words to express their lived truth; they sustained their faith by reconciling experience. With courage, they changed, having recognized that experience demanded it. And by their example, we find that the Fourth Gospel also represents something far more "different" than we, over the course of time, have allowed.

Yet from the perspective of our shared human experience, the themes spilling from the pages of the Fourth Gospel represent the very opposite of difference. The grief that culminates in John chapter 17, and the gifts of faith, freedom, grace, and love, weave their way into all forms of literature and artistry. Here we will explore three poems, three poetic moments of Johannine inspiration, that communicate an experience of God's presence, that affirm our shared search for freedom, grace, and love in the midst of difficulty and change.

High above the rest of John, above the seven signs of the earlier chapters and above the passion and resurrection of the last, there lies the strangest moonscape in the Scripture, and so in all literature, and so in life. I refer to John chapters 13 to 17. We are about to place our exegetical flag on the very summit, the highest of high peaks, the textual Matterhorn, Everest, Mount Washington, Pike's Peak: John 17:3.

"And this is eternal life, that they may know you, the only true God, and Jesus Christ whom you have sent."

I. Where We Least Expect to Find It: Freedom in Disappointment, Grace in Dislocation, Love in Departure

1. Brother John

We are four siblings in my family of origin. The older three have brown hair. The youngest, whose name is John, is a redhead. John's bright red locks are unlike—quite unlike—the less remarkable curls of Bob, Cathy, and Cynthia. He stands apart,

---

3. Brown, *Community of the Beloved Disciple,* 90–91.

does John, with such a distinctive aspect. It makes you wonder where he came from.

In such difference, my brother John is like that of his Gospel namesake, the Fourth Gospel. St. John, the "youngest" of the four, stands out as different from his Synoptic siblings Matthew, Mark, and Luke. They three—with their shared parables and teachings, their shared emphasis on Jesus' humanity, their shared trips from Galilee to Jerusalem, which we might cheekily name their shared brown hair—just don't look at all like their redheaded younger brother.

Growing up, we would occasionally attend the family reunion held for one part of our tribe. You may have done the same in your family. Like yours, perhaps, ours is something of a predictable affair. During the summer, we assemble on a farm near Albany, a farm which has been in the family since before George Washington rode a horse. After the usual light meal of beef, corn, potatoes, bread, sausage, pies, pickles, and so on, the extended family (or those who, having eaten so, can still move) will sometimes stand for a photograph on the long farmhouse veranda. Perhaps you can guess what it shows: out of eighty people, about sixty—young and old, tall and short, heavy and slight, male and female—have red hair, like John. Three-quarters are redheads. In fact, the photo looks to be a sea of red hair; maybe a redhead's convention out in the farm fields of Cooperstown, New York. My brother John isn't the oddball; his siblings are.

St. John is not the second-century Greco-Roman oddball. His Synoptic siblings are. When you put the Fourth Gospel, with all its red-haired radical difference, on the family farmhouse veranda of second-century religious literature, it fits right in. John, especially in these late chapters, stands shoulder to shoulder with all the Gnostic writings that are so like his. It looks like a redhead's convention. He looks and sounds quite like the rest of his second and third cousins, once or twice removed, such as The Paraphrase of Shem, the Treatise on the Resurrection, the Odes of Solomon, the Apocryphon of John, the Gospel of Peter, the Gospel of Mary. How else will we ever hear this voice of Jesus from John 17:3?

"And this is eternal life, that they may know you, the only true God, and Jesus Christ whom you have sent."

Six differences! Six differences set John apart from his Synoptic siblings. John speaks of eternal life, not kingdom of heaven. Know, not believe. The only true God, not Abba. Jesus Christ, not Rabbi or Master. Sent, not begotten.

This voice is nothing—nothing—like the voice of the Sermon on the Mount, or that of the parable of the Good Samaritan, or that of the cry from Psalm 22 on the cross. Not human, but divine, here. Not earthly, but heavenly, here. Not low, but high, here. Not immanent, but transcendent, here.

The community of the Gospel of John had a radical experience of Jesus, as God on earth. To render that experience meaningful, they had the radical courage to embrace language from heretics, the Gnostics around them, to use as their own. They did so because this language fit. It rang true. It validated their lived experience of divine grace and divine freedom in Jesus. For these huddled humans clinging to Christ, the sense of consecration they had found—the sense of holy living and dying, the sense of consecrated joy—was rendered in the Light of the World, in the Bread of Life, in the Good Shepherd, in the Resurrection, in the Word made flesh.

Raymond Brown explained it this way:

> Some scholars may ponder on the luck of the Beloved Disciple that his community's Gospel was not recognized for the sectarian tractate that it really was. But others among us will see this as a recognition by Apostolic Christians that the Johannine language was not really a riddle and the Johannine voice was not alien... What the Johannine Christians considered to be a tradition that had come down from Jesus seems to have been accepted by many other Christians as *an embraceable variant* of the tradition that they had from Jesus.[4]

The community of the Gospel of John feared not the culture around them. They feared not truth, not even truth expressed

---

4. Brown, *Community of the Beloved Disciple*, 90–91. (Emphasis mine.)

outside of their particular religious circle. They had the guts to adopt the language of pagans, outsiders, heretics, Gnostics, to celebrate and consecrate their faith. In doing so, John's community opened up the church to the world, to the future, to the culture around them. They changed their way of speaking of Christ, and pointed to Christ above, within, and around them, transforming the culture. They changed. They had the courage to change.

In our own age, when the Gospel of John served raw, without cooking—which is to say, without historical interpretation—can be made to sound like the voice not of tradition but of traditionalism, we do well to remember John's courage to change, to reach out to the culture around, to put the gospel in word and music on the air waves of a secular culture, and, where possible, to use that same culture.

2. John

The Gospel and the Letters named for John were given their shared name long ago, in the second century, by a person whom once we termed a "church father" but whom we would now call an "early Christian writer." John's Jesus makes several remarkable claims. Are many of them historically reliable? No. They reflect a changed understanding of the Christ, hard-won and hard-earned.

John's community had suffered trauma, and trauma brings change. In the late first century, a painful separation between groups of Jewish and Gentile Christians gave rise to passages in John that we may understand, historically and theologically, as a particularly dark moment in the Christian tradition of anti-Semitism. The community behind John contended with those whom they called "the Jews," even though they, the Jews, were their own kin. Together with this conflict, John's community suffered the trauma of disappointment. They suffered the trauma of dislocation. And, *mirable dictu,* in the cross of Christ and in the loss of John, this ancient faith community uncovered a way to love.

John's community knew about disappointment. They had, for three generations, awaited the realization of the primitive hope of the church. They awaited the return of Christ; the resurrection of the dead from their graves; the end of time; the apocalypse of God. It did not come. He did not come, at least not in the way once hoped. They found the courage to admit it, and change. The most remarkable feature of the New Testament is that John, rather than losing himself in a sea of disheartening failure—in the very eye of his most stormy theological hurricane—found freedom. In theological disappointment, he found freedom.

John's community knew about dislocation. They had been thrown out of their religious home—de-synagogued, if you will—and wandered out in the street, as it were. The life they grew up with had cast them out; they lost their mother tongue, mother land, mother tradition. They found the courage to face it, and change. It took three generations for them to grasp a joyful grace in dislocation. Paul, who likely did not write of or know John, might well have said: *See? I told you, "When I am weak, then I am strong."*[5] Count it all grace, brethren, when various dislocations beset you!

John's community knew about departure. The layers of grief culminating in chapter 17, while ostensibly a rehearsal of Jesus's own departure, may also have been crafted by the heart and voice of their aged John, the other and beloved disciple, whose own departure in the midst of disappointment and dislocation itself provoked new layers of grief. Is it not ironic that the sharpest, most rarified language of love in all of the New Testament—in all of literature—arises in the hour of departure?

Your own participation in this study is cordially invited. Look back at all your experience to date. What is your greatest disappointment? It is a clue to freedom. What is your hardest dislocation? It is a signpost for grace. What is your most grievous departure? It is the way of love.

The measures of freedom and grace given to us become real possibilities—real freedom and real grace—only when we have the gracious freedom to decide for faith. The same is magnificently true of love. This is the message of John, at the end.

---

5. 2 Cor 12:10, NRSV.

But how does this happen? Freedom, grace, and love come through variance, in John; difference, in John; the courage to act and think differently, in John. Let us examine variance from different perspectives.

3. Freedom In Disappointment, Grace in Dislocation, Love in Departure: Today

a. Freedom

A poor man went to worship at a Methodist church. The congregation welcomed him, and he returned week by week. After a while, the church community took up a collection and bought him a nice new suit, with a blue tie. He happily received the gift, but they never saw him in church again. The congregation was disappointed to lose their new member.

Sometime later, on the street, one of the church members saw him and asked what had happened. Did he not like the suit? Did it not fit? Was he afraid to wear it?

"Oh, no," came the reply. "I love the suit. I look great in it. I saw myself in the mirror and thought, 'I look like a million bucks. I look too good to go to the Methodist church. I think I'm dressed well enough to go the Episcopal church. I'm going to go there.' And that is what I did." Disappointment, coinciding with freedom!

The freedom of the gospel has gradually embraced multiple variants. The poor. The immigrant. People of color. Those once enslaved. Women. Gay people. Others. The Other. In fact, the lesson of grace enshrined in John, and taught through the throes of dislocation, is the spiritual expansion of grace found in the embrace of the embraceable variant.

From John's theological disappointment came freedom. In our time, speaking of theological disappointment, we are bidding a reluctant farewell to God. To a certain, junior, perception of God. God reigns. This we affirm, with the church militant and triumphant. But in a secular world, God's way among us is, disappointingly, away from us. *He is risen. He is not here. See the place where they laid him.* And you?

Pasternak loved Shakespeare's Sonnet 66. It is said that whenever he read aloud, the crowd would not let him leave until he had rehearsed it for them. "Give us the 66th . . ." Its evocation of daily anxiety bears remembering. The poem is unequaled in its announcement of disappointment, but also in its freedom to wrestle with it.

When life gives you the 66th remember Shakespeare, but remember especially his last couplet. "Captive good attending captain ill . . ." Can you hear that? It begs to be heard. Stand with your people in tragedy, honest and kind in word and deed.

b. Grace

Some years ago, we sat at dinner with several other couples, in a beautiful home, over a majestic meal graciously served. Because the couples knew each other well, and were in trust to each other, there was the chance for hard and serious conversation—consecrated conversation, you might say. This evening, the debate swirled around gay marriage.

There are tipping points in the way a culture moves. Some of them occur at dinner, in beautiful homes, over majestic meals graciously served. The host was opposed—to gay marriage, that is. The conversation widened, and then narrowed, and then widened again. We can surely agree that there are many ways of keeping faith, and many honest, different, points of view, on this and on many issues.

Across the table sat Carol, mother of two fine teenagers, married with joy to a business leader, baseball player, Red Sox fan. She had battled cancer once before, and now it had returned, and she fought it again. We could not see it then, but in seven months she would be gone.

Through some heat and some laughter, much disagreement but little discord, the conversation, consecrated you might say, continued. Carol spoke openly, and at one point said: "You know, I have learned how precious, how fragile life is, what a gift every day is. Here is what I feel: if two people truly love each other, deeply commit to each other, and want to consecrate their vows—that is, they want what Doug and I have—why would I ever want to stand in their way? Why would I ever want to deprive them of that happiness that I know so well?" I heard some minds changing as the dessert came out. The embodiment of the embraceable variant.

In our time, we have—as has every generation, as did the generation of the Beloved Disciple—known sociological dislocation aplenty. Our churches are, and have been for decades, in the throes of dislocation. Lyle Schaller had our number a quarter century ago when he identified change as the primary need for most congregations and denominations.[6] "Reversing a period of numerical decline requires changes," wrote Schaller;[7] yet denominations continue to accept an annual decline in membership in exchange for the tacit agreement that there be no significant change. And so, in the time since Schaller's message, United Methodism has lost fifty percent of its Northeast membership. Today, of the more than 800 pulpits in my home conference, Upper New York,[8] perhaps two-thirds are occupied by non-elders: the preaching and ministry are done by people without full or proper education, preparation, examination, or ordination. In what other sector of serious life would we permit this?

In grace, our healthy future will come from a resurrection: of thought, word, and deed; of traditional worship; of traveling elders who excel in preaching; and in tithing to support the church we love. All these are found in the healthy life of healthy, vibrant, discreet communities of faith. To change, to admit the need for change, to have the courage to change, is to live biblical grace in a modern life.

---

6. Schaller, *Strategies for Change*, 10.

7. Schaller, *Strategies for Change*, 11.

8. The UMC Online Directory & Statistics website (http://www.umdata.org/SearchChurches.aspx) reported 826 churches in the Upper New York Conference in 2021, the latest year for which data was available.

Our New England poet recognized the power of intentional choice.

The Road Not Taken

Two roads diverged in a yellow wood,
And sorry I could not travel both
And be one traveler, long I stood
And looked down one as far as I could
To where it bent in the undergrowth;
Then took the other, as just as fair,
And having perhaps the better claim,
Because it was grassy and wanted wear;
Though as for that the passing there
Had worn them really about the same,
And both that morning equally lay
In leaves no step had trodden black.
Oh, I kept the first for another day!
Yet knowing how way leads on to way,
I doubted if I should ever come back.
I shall be telling this with a sigh
Somewhere ages and ages hence:
Two roads diverged in a wood, and I—
I took the one less traveled by,
And that has made all the difference.[9]

I bear witness—all the lastingly good features of my life have come through grace in dislocation: name in baptism, faith in confirmation, community in Eucharist, partnership in marriage, work in ordination, love in pardon, and hope in Christ, for this life and the next. In our dislocation we discover grace—an embraceable variant—which makes all the difference.

---

9. Frost, *Complete Poems*, 105.

c. Love

"There is nothing that can replace the absence of someone dear to us,"[10] wrote Bonhoeffer. The departure of the Christ makes space for love. "Just as I have loved you, you also should love one another."[11] And you?

In our time, we face loss, we face the departure of persons and groups. When we buried Lu Lingzi, our BU student who died in the bombing of the 2013 Boston Marathon, her family bowed, ceremonially and from the waist, at the very close of the service. A recognition of real love in real departure.

Sometimes a dose of realized eschatology can clear the mind and strengthen the soul. In a way, every day is our last. In a way, heaven and hell are here and now. In a way, the end time is all of time. John puts it this way: "the hour is coming, *and is now here.*"[12]

"Discipline yourselves, keep alert. Like a roaring lion your adversary the devil prowls around, looking for someone to devour."[13] We may shed the inherited demonic mythology in the verse, knowing and honoring its origins in the distant past, yet nonetheless we fully recognize the spiritual truth here: we know not what a day may bring, but only that the hour for serving is always present.

> O LORD, you have searched me and known me.
> You know when I sit down and when I rise up;
> > you discern my thoughts from far away.
> You search out my path and my lying down,
> > and are acquainted with all my ways.
> Even before a word is on my tongue,
> > O LORD, you know it completely.
> You hem me in, behind and before,
> > and lay your hand upon me.

---

10. Bonhoeffer, *Letters and Papers*, 238.
11. John 13:34, NRSV.
12. John 4:23, NRSV. (Emphasis mine.)
13. 1 Pet 5:8, NRSV.

> Such knowledge is too wonderful for me;
> > it is so high that I cannot attain it.
> Where can I go from your Spirit?
> > Or where can I flee from your presence?
> If I ascend to heaven, you are there;
> > if I make my bed in Sheol, you are there.
> If I take the wings of the morning
> > and settle at the farthest limits of the sea,
> even there your hand shall lead me,
> > and your right hand shall hold me fast.
> If I say, "Surely the darkness shall cover me,
> > and the light around me become night,"
> even the darkness is not dark to you;
> > the night is bright as the day,
> > for darkness is as light to you.[14]

We, too, want to discipline ourselves and keep alert. So we pray. (Do you pray?) So we commune. (Do you receive the Eucharist?) So we study. (Have you devotionally read your Bible this week?) So we converse with one another. (Have you opened home and heart recently in Christian conversation?) So we fast—park your car, save your money, do not "reply all," fight pollution and debt and dehumanization. We, too, want to discipline ourselves and keep alert. We want to live a life of love that will, in departure, deliver us.

"New occasions teach new duties; Time makes ancient good uncouth; / They must upward still, and onward, who would keep abreast of Truth."[15] *Sursum corda:* lift up your hearts! The variance, your distinctive self, is utterly embraceable. That variance, and your courage to live it, bring saving wholeness.

There is a clue to *freedom* in disappointment. There is a signpost to *grace* in dislocation. There is a way of *love* in departure. The community of the Beloved Disciple showed us so. "And this

---

14. Ps 139:1–12, NRSV.
15. Lowell, "Present Crisis," st. 18.

is eternal life, that they may know you, the only true God, and Jesus Christ whom you have sent."

II. A Johannine Inspiration

From the doors of Marsh Chapel emerges, every spring, a class of soon-to-be preachers, holding Bibles in their right hands and massive debt in their left. By the first of July, many of them are in pulpits preaching; they might preach, every Sunday, a Sunday sermon "about God and about twenty minutes," for forty subsequent years. Some of those sermons will come from John.

Come Saturday night they will begin to write their sermons. They will find in the passages to be read from John various troubling, troublesome, troublous passages. It is only a diachronic reading of John—one that looks at its place and time, its community of origin, its *sitz im leben*—which frees, and which alone can give a measure of the promise that "you will know the truth, and the truth will make you free."[16] One hopes that our students will have acquired, in addition to their diploma and their debt, some pious understanding of John's history and theology.

Well. Don't you know that life is a funny old dog? For six years, I had alongside me as teaching assistant a most brilliant, funny, Episcopal priest and mother of two. She is a literary critic. She practices rhetorical criticism. She loves poetry, and the Johannine literature has long inspired poetry. Twice per term, she brought her exotic medicines, the alchemic mixtures of literary criticism, to bear on our text. (I like to be magnanimous, don't you know. I believe in the liberal balance, don't you know. I honor freedom of speech in the university, don't you know. Plus, the students loved her. They appreciated her approach—*as an addition, mind you, to the main work of the course*—and I too appreciate her and love her work. Even teachers can learn. It was that great Yankee Yogi Berra who said, "You can observe a lot by just watching." Or, as the nursery rhyme goes, "There was an owl liv'd in an oak / The

---

16. John 8:32, NRSV.

more he heard, the less he spoke / The less he spoke, the more he heard. / O, if men were all like that wise bird.")

The Reverend, now Reverend Doctor, Regina Walton showed our students poems which grow out of the Fourth Gospel and illumine its meaning. For this exercise, I determined to show them to you, as well. They are light, joy, truth, power, meaning, and love. They are Gospel. They are beautiful. They are rhetorically beautiful religious language—what other than such beauty will drive out the demons of hateful religious rhetoric?—and they can help us here, today.

1. George Herbert, "The Call"

The poet George Herbert (1593-1633)[17] knew from a young age that he was called to write devotional poetry. Herbert was an orator at Cambridge, and later a priest. He knew John Donne, who was a family friend. His work employs both trochaic and iambic meters. He writes, among other things, of the soul's call to God, and of the claim the believer has on God. That is, in his work there is a Johannine courage. One of his most famous works expresses it: "Love bade me welcome: yet my soul drew back . . . / You must sit down, sayes Love, and taste my meat: / So I did sit and eat."[18] Herbert wrote of love.

His poem "The Call" draws on John 14:17, John 6:6, and John 16:22.

> The Call
> Come, my Way, my Truth, my Life:
> Such a Way, as gives us breath:
> Such a Truth, as ends all strife:
> And such a Life, as killeth death.
> Come, my Light, my Feast, my Strength:
> Such a Light, as shows a feast:
> Such a Feast, as mends in length:

---

17. Encyclopedia Britannica Online, s.v. "George Herbert."
18. Herbert, *The Temple*, 227-8.

Such a Strength, as makes his guest.
Come, my Joy, my Love, my Heart:
Such a Joy, as none can move:
Such a Love, as none can part:
Such a Heart, as joyes in love.[19]

Such a heart as joyes in love. As a pastor in the Marsh Chapel community, I have the privilege of seeing women and men struggling to live in faith and doing so by inspiration. In our community we expect a birth or two, fairly soon, a joy in love. In our community we have couples who are in the throes of making marriage work and work better, a joy in love. In our community we have dads and moms who pray for the safe returns of their children in armed service, a joy in love. In our community we have some who struggle with the physical and personal challenges of aging, and find healing care, a joy in love. In our community we have students learning not someone else's fantasy of what they might learn but what they most want to learn, a joy in love. In our community we have people, the salt of the earth, who reflect and radiate Christ's joy in love.

2. Henry Vaughan, "The Night"

The Welsh poet Henry Vaughan (1622–1695) lived during a dark time in English history,[20] a time rife with war, political turmoil, and religious intolerance. The King was understood to be anointed by God. Vaughan fought for the Royalists during the English Civil Wars. Following the execution of Charles I in 1649, the Church of England was disestablished, and the Book of Common Prayer was outlawed.[21]

Vaughan is known as one of Herbert's most ardent followers and admirers, crediting Herbert for his own turn to religious poetry. Vaughan's poetry evokes his time. He recalls the great

---

19. Herbert, *The Temple*, 187.
20. Encyclopedia Britannica Online, s.v. "Henry Vaughan."
21. The English Church and the monarchy were reinstated in 1660.

Pseudo-Dionysus and *The Cloud of Unknowing*. He celebrates night and the darkness of God in a way that I believe connects truly to our time, as well.

"The Night" is Vaughan's poem based on Nicodemus at night, as found in John 3: "[Nicodemus] came to Jesus by night and said to him, 'Rabbi, we know that you are a teacher who has come from God; for no one can do these signs that you do apart from the presence of God.'"[22] Here some verses from this wondrous work.

> The Night
> > Through that pure Virgin shrine,
> That sacred veil drawn o'er thy glorious noon,
> That men might look and live as Glow-worms shine,
> > And face the Moon:
> Wise Nicodemus saw such light
> As made him know his God by night.
> > Most blest believer he!
> Who in that land of darkness and blind eyes
> Thy long-expected healing wings could see,
> > When thou didst rise!
> And, what can never more be done,
> Did at midnight speak with the Sun!
>
> > O who will tell me, where
> He found thee at that dead and silent hour?
> What hallowed solitary ground did bear
> > So rare a flower,
> Within whose sacred leaves did lie
> The fulness of the Deity?
>
> > . . . .
>
> > Dear night! this world's defeat;
> The stop to busy fools; care's check and curb;
> The day of Spirits; my soul's calm retreat
> > Which none disturb!
> Christ's progress, and his prayer time;

22. John 3:2, NRSV.

> The hours to which high Heaven doth chime.
> . . . .
> Were all my loud, evil days
> Calm and unhaunted as is thy dark Tent,
> Whose peace but by some Angel's wing or voice
> Is seldom rent;
> Then I in Heaven all the long year
> Would keep, and never wander here.
> But living where the Sun
> Doth all things wake, and where all mix and tire
> Themselves and others, I consent and run
> To ev'ry mire,
> And by this world's ill-guiding light,
> Err more than I can do by night.
> There is in God (some say)
> A deep but dazzling darkness; As men here
> Say it is late and dusky, because they
> See not all clear;
> O for that night! where I in him
> Might live invisible and dim.[23]

Most blest believer he! Who in that land of darkness and blind eyes thy long-expected healing wings could see. Nicodemus—like the Beloved Disciple, like the Paraclete, like the Logos, like the "Judeans"—helps form a bridge from the community of faith to the community of life, from religion to culture, from church to world. And back.

At Marsh Chapel, we yearn for a faith amenable to culture and a culture amenable to faith. We desire such not because it is immediately present or likely to arise in our time with ease—it is not, and it will not—but because it is right and true. We hope

---

23. Vaughan, "The Night," 55–56. Text and syntax here updated to modern English for clarity.

for such, to paraphrase Vaclav Havel, not just because it stands a chance to succeed, but because it is good.[24]

When the faith you personally cherish walks by night, without fear, across this whole great land, and when the culture you inhabit visits the community of faith, without fear, by night or day—when Jesus and Nicodemus embrace—then a bit of heaven has come to earth. When, for example, as happened some time ago, the salt and light of the Marsh Chapel Choir finds purchase in a great hall with a culturally iconic band—a band not particularly known for religious observance, by the way (the Rolling Stones)—then you have an apocalyptic moment, a place of faith amenable to culture and culture amenable to faith.

3. T.S. Eliot. "Ash Wednesday"

You will not be surprised by the choice for our third poet. The poet T.S. Eliot was born in America but lived most of his life in England, until his death in 1965.[25] He was, arguably, the greatest poet of his age, and one of the greatest of any age. While our generation does not cling to him as did an earlier one—and this itself is a pity—he nonetheless touches us, too. To him we owe the rediscovery of the metaphysical poets.

Eliot found God's presence in God's absence. Like Herbert's mature claim upon God, like Vaughan's love of night, Eliot's presence in absence seems strikingly close to the spirit of our own age. His poem "Ash Wednesday" owes much to the first verse of the Gospel of John: "In the beginning was the Word, and the Word was with God, and the Word was God."[26] In the spirit of presence in absence, this poem is not printed here; I ask you to find a copy, and savor it.

---

24. Havel, *Peace*, 181. "Hope, in this deep and powerful sense, is not the same as joy that things are going well, or willingness to invest in enterprises that are obviously headed for early success, but, rather, an ability to work for something because it is good, not just because it stands a chance to succeed."

25. Encyclopedia Britannica Online, s.v. "T.S. Eliot."

26. John 1:1, NRSV.

"The Word within the world and for the world," writes Eliot. At Marsh Chapel in Boston, we honor and celebrate our strongest sister pulpits in the north: Asbury First in Rochester, New York; Christ Church in New York City; Foundry Church in Washington, D.C. Over the coming decades, we shall need these four arrows together in a quiver—Marsh, Asbury, Christ, Foundry—as we minister the Word within the world and for the world. Superintending is rooted in 1 John, but the vocal leadership, the spiritual leadership, the Spirit, is rooted in John.

In Methodism, our pulpits—since Wesley, Asbury, Cartwright, Shaw, Sockman, Tittle, and all—have historically led the way. Now, in our time of ecclesiological fragmentation much farther advanced than most realize, we shall need to rely not so heavily, and certainly not exclusively, on the superintending voices—important as they are—but on the deeper streams of mercy still fed by the healthy communities of faith and by their pulpits. Wesley loved the Eastern Orthodox traditions—Alexandria, Jerusalem, Antioch, Constantinople—those of the patriarchies, rather than those of the bishops of Rome and elsewhere. The communities in the East led, and lead. We need to look East, in this sense; we need to listen first to the remaining vibrant pulpits.

Within all forms of artistry, wherever they may appear, the themes of John's Gospel are recognizable because they reflect our shared experience of the presence of God. In John, we find difference—the trauma of change; the conflict between groups; the pain of disappointment, dislocation, and departure—but we also, miraculously, find the way to freedom, to grace, to love. The liberal biblical theology that resides in John recognizes the need for change and the call for variance.

Here we saw three poems, three moments of Johannine inspiration, from Herbert, Vaughan, and Eliot. One for those in need, celebrating the One who joyes in love. One for those at night, celebrating the one who marries faith and life. One for those troubled by absence, celebrating the coming, the return of voice and word. Amen. Amen. Amen. *Beloved, let us love one another!*[27]

---

27. 1 John 4:7, NRSV.

7

The Difference Easter Makes

THE BOSTON MARATHON IS held every Spring, in April. If one attempted to run it—all 26.2 miles across some grueling ascents, one in particular named "Heartbreak Hill"—without any conditioning, without any readiness, you can imagine how they might fare. Some preparation, then, is necessary.

So it goes with a most compelling exercise in liberal, biblical theology that arrives every Spring, as the church gathers for the feast of Easter. The exercises inevitably come, year by year, as Lent gives way to Holy Week, and the sunrise of Easter morning approaches. Some preparation is necessary to strengthen our spiritual selves, to stretch our awareness, and to run these annual exercises.

Easter, by its very mystery, wonder, inexpressibility, rapture, and delight, evokes a reliance upon a liberal biblical theology. The New Testament carries no fewer than three accounts of Jesus's resurrection; accounts that convey different events and emphases, each truthfully told by the witness who lived it. The resurrection is a mystery, proclaims Paul[1]; yet at the center of all accounts is the notion that something important happened, something powerful and transformative that had a powerful and transformative

---

1. 1 Cor 15:51, NRSV.

effect on those who experienced it. We grant the differences of experience because we understand that the responses found in the heart of the Easter gospel are meant to explain *who* and *why*, not *what* and *how*. To seek, among our diverse experiences with resurrection, the commonality of its sweeping, infinite effects: such is the liberal biblical theology offered by the Easter gospel.

Easter calls us to a life of faith, and we respond by running the marathon of faithful life, with all its grueling ascents and its heartbreaking hills. But year by year, a thoughtful approach to the Easter exercise can build our faith, our strength, for the challenges to come.

One's approach to and rendering of the Easter gospel is a defining point in teaching, preaching, and ministry. Here follow a variety of ways of approach. In these sermonic paragraphs of exercise, preparation, and engagement, one may "practice the presence of God"[2] in the cadence of the Easter Gospel. Let us respond to Easter in worship, in history, and in life. Let us meditate on the question of heaven and the mystery of resurrection. Let us hear the voices of those who would share their diverse experiences of resurrection to join us in partnership in the gospel.

The Lord is Risen! He is risen, indeed!

I. Responding in Worship

Let us respond to Easter in worship: hearing the Easter word, hearing the Easter hymns, singing together with full voice and heart, greeting each other with a Methodist handshake. We yearn for the worship of Easter morning.

Others, too, have known the yearning of, and for, worship. The beloved community which gave birth to the Fourth Gospel did so. Let your imagination take you, for a moment, to a borrowed upper room—in Ephesus, say, around the year AD 90. Candles burn. A meal has been offered and received. Among the fifty or so there present, there descends a gradual settling, a quiet. Acute pain

---

2. Lawrence, *Practice of the Presence of God*.

abides in this circle: the pain of the loss of a beloved leader; the pain of the loss of a venerable religious lineage; the pain of the loss of a prized eschatological hope. Love, faith, and hope, all lost.

As the circle settles, after a prayer and reading and a further silence and a long hymn sung, *The One who has held them . . . speaks*. Imagine the early church, small and struggling, in worship. In the silence and in the singing and then in the mournful, joyful, worship antiphon. Were these Gospel words first sung?

I am . . . light, life, resurrection, way, gate, good shepherd, bread, water.[3]

I am . . . the true vine. You will know the truth. That they may know you, the only true God.[4]

Every heart has secret sorrows. We feel them now, in our time. Every land has cavernous grief. We feel it now, in our time. Back in those ancient days, for the antiphonal singers of our scripture, the hurts were dislocation, disappointment, and departure. And they named them. Can you name yours? Have you named your hurt?

Hear the Easter antiphon: "Abide in me as I abide in you."[5] Stay. Remain. Settle. Dig in. Locate. Vines take a long time to grow. But so?

John's portrait of Jesus "arose from his constant awareness, which he shared with the members of his community, that they were living in the presence of the Glorified One. So dazzling was this glory that any memory of a less-than-glorious Christ was altogether eclipsed."[6]

A dazzling glory alongside a grievous hurt. With the ancient beloved community, can you lift a muted alleluia? Every hymn, for all its joy, carries a guttural memory of acute hurt. In worship, today, can you pray with joy, while still remembering the brokenness out of which that alleluia comes? Let Charles Wesley, let

---

3. John 8:12; John 11:25; John 14:6; John 10:11; John 10:9; John 6:35, NRSV.
4. John 15:1; John 8:32; John 17:3, NRSV.
5. John 15:4, NRSV.
6. Ashton, *Gospel of John*, 198.

Charles Tindley, let the suffering of your own ancestral family's older past guide you.

Let us respond to Easter in worship.

II. Responding in History

Let us respond to Easter in history.

What is our place in history, our communal responsibility in real time? A surface glide across Holy Scripture will not allow, cannot provide, gospel insight. You want to sift the Scriptures. You want to know them inside and out, upside and down, through and through and through; and then, it may be, by happenstance or grace or the clumsy luck of a very human preacher, you may hear a steadying, saving word.

Through some Easter seasons, you have perhaps noticed, noted, or winced to hear the Letter of John—1 John—amending, redacting, muting, and amplifying the Gospel of John. You are keen listeners, practiced and adroit, so you will have wondered a bit about this. Why does 1 John nip at the heels of John?

The two "books," John and 1 John, were likely written by different authors, in different decades, in different circumstances, with different motives. The Gospel acclaims Spirit. The Letter concentrates on work, ethics, morals, community, tradition, leadership, and judgment from higher authority rather than judgment by belief and by believer. We may just have, it is important to say, the Gospel—with all its radicality—as part of the New Testament because of its brother-named letter vouching, as it were, for the sanity of the Gospel. The letter, like James James Morrison Morrison Weatherby George Dupree, takes great care of its Gospel mother, the very cat's mother, you see.[7]

The Gospel revealed the Spirit—elsewhere called Paraclete or Advocate—come upon us and received, and, with it, the

---

7. A reference to A. A. Milne's tongue-in-cheek poem "Disobedience" (1924), in which a three-year-old boy named James James Morrison Morrison Weatherby George Dupree expects his adult mother to follow his safety directive, which is meant to take "great care" of her.

forgiveness of sins.[8] But at the heels, nipping, comes along 1 John, which names the Paraclete or Advocate not as Spirit but as Jesus Christ the righteous,[9] whose commandments all believers are to keep on pain of disobedience become lying, and truth taken flight. Both read on the same Sunday within minutes of each other, even as they face each other in loving disagreement.

As the Gospel alleluia still lingered with the Lord and God risen, the Letter—on the *qui vive* and on the attack—spelled out again, in no uncertain terms, that the righteous do the right,[10] that "handsome is as handsome does," so to speak. Both read on the same Sunday, within minutes of each other, even as they face each other in loving disagreement.

The Gospel acclaimed the pastoral image of the good shepherd[11]—whose one glorification on the cross is meant to obliterate the need of any other such—even as the worried Letter worried out a long and sorry recollection of Abel's one-time brother Cain, and the demands of love from one who laid down his life, with whom and for whom we are then meant to do something of the same.[12] "Let us love, not in word or speech, but in truth and action,"[13] says the Letter, when the whole of the Gospel says simply "love," says that words outlast deeds, and that speech, the speech of the glorious Risen, ever routs works. Both read on the same Sunday within minutes of each other, even as they face each other in loving disagreement.

When and where the Gospel, our "Spiritual Gospel," counsels "abide"[14] and remain, the Letter—fearing antinomian abandon—appends to its own most beautiful love poem the charge, again, of lying;[15] now also of lack of brotherly love and of schism, these

8. John 20:22–23, NRSV.
9. 1 John 2:1, NRSV.
10. 1 John 3:4–10, NRSV.
11. John 10:1–18, NRSV.
12. 1 John 3:12–17, NRSV.
13. 1 John 3:18, NRSV.
14. John 15, NRSV.
15. 1 John 4:21, NRSV.

which surely prompted this very letter as the spiritualists and the traditionalists, the Gnostics and the ethicists, parted company: one toward the free land of Montanus and Marcion; the other toward Rome and the emerging church, victorious but against that which the Gospel was born, bred, written, and preached. Both read on the same Sunday within minutes of each other, even as they face each other in loving disagreement.

Both are right, of course. We would not otherwise still need or read them, let alone together. But you are right, too, to feel some neck pain, some whiplash, as Gospel soars and Letter deflates. It is as if the Song of Solomon were being sung by Obadiah.

The blessed Scripture bears incontrovertible, conflicted witness. Easter is a conflicted—and so, muted—alleluia, and was so already twenty centuries ago, as the resurrection cross of Jesus was raised up in mournful joy, a real joy made real by its honesty about sorrow. Real joy becomes real by its honesty about sorrow. *To move out of strife and into joy, we shall need honesty about what, and about whom, we have lost.* The Scripture, read hard and deep, can help us. For history, including—and perhaps especially including—religious history, is endless contention and intractable difference.

To respond to Easter in history will mean, for you, bearing the cross of endless contention and intractable difference, and laboring daily to reconcile history and community, effort in which the best of intentions run afoul of circumstance or chance. And, more, it means that you, as a person of faith, may well encounter a discrete time to say something or do something—a time when some somewhat risky and uncomfortable mode of social involvement, or existential engagement, will beckon you.

Let us respond to Easter in history.

III. Responding in Life

Let us respond to Easter in life.

The Gospel prepares us for the lifelong work of responding to Easter. The Gospel tells about resurrection largely on the basis of experience. Experience and troubles—troubles that provoked lasting questions.

The Gospels and Letters respond in life to Easter, in a muted alleluia, in a sober acclamation. *The church is alive,* they acclaim.

We may have a powerful experience of the church alive across the river of death, especially when we come to celebrate the life of a dear sister or brother in faith. The church is the body of Christ. We affirm a bodily, physical resurrection, tasted for a time in church. I give you Emily Dickinson:[16]

> This World is not Conclusion.
> A Species stands beyond —
> Invisible, as Music —
> But positive, as Sound —
> It beckons, and it baffles —
> Philosophy — don't know —
> And through a Riddle, at the last —
> Sagacity must go —
> To guess it, puzzles scholars —
> To gain it, Men have borne
> Contempt of Generations
> And Crucifixion, shown —
> Faith slips — and laughs, and rallies —
> Blushes, if any see —
> Plucks at a twig of Evidence —
> And asks a Vane, the way —
> Much Gesture, from the Pulpit —
> Strong Hallelujahs roll —
> Narcotics cannot still the Tooth
> That nibbles at the soul —

Or, as one of our wise-beyond-years undergraduates said one spring, "I will be careful with any kind of hope that I have."

---

16. Dickinson, "This World is not Conclusion," 171.

The future is open, acclaim the Gospel and Letters. That is: there is a spiritual resurrection in your future.

I once met a psychiatrist who said his work was to offer the possibility that stories might have a different ending. You know that story of your life at its worst, the story with the same ending no matter how you live and how you tell it? That story can have a different ending, another conclusion. It can.

Your repeated narrative of inherited addiction can be overcome in sobriety.

Your religious amnesia about what is fun in faith—giving and inviting—can be lifted like a fog at dawn, and you can sing out your soul.

Your civic inheritance, a disregard for the limits of power, can be overcome in a more collegial, humbler, more mature foreign policy. Your usurpation can give way to response. Your isolation can give way to community. Your imperialism can give way to justice. We can learn lessons from our experience.

The seemingly unending grind, of employment and unemployment, love and loss, relationship and rejection, can change. Things can, and will in Christ, be better for you and for us. The cycle can be broken, when what is in place is invaded by what is taking place.

Love is real, they acclaim, both Gospel and Letter. In this way, at least for once, the Letter surpasses the Gospel, the child outdoes the parent:

> Beloved, let us love one another, because love is from God; everyone who loves is born of God and knows God. Whoever does not love does not know God, for God is love. God's love was revealed among us in this way: God sent his only Son into the world so that we might live through him. In this is love, not that we loved God but that he loved us and sent his Son to be the atoning sacrifice for our sins. Beloved, since God loved us so much, we also ought to love one another. No one has ever seen

God; if we love one another, God lives in us, and his love is perfected in us.[17]

Who would, or could, or should, say more?

Let us respond to Easter in life. The church is alive. The future is open. Love fills the heart. In these truths we find foretastes of heaven. If the heavenly banquet offers this menu, perhaps we need, over these few earthly years, to acquire a certain taste for certain things: faith and hope and love.

May we respond to Easter in worship, in history, and in life? It is an Easter call to the altar. It is your Easter altar call.

IV. Responding to the Question of Heaven

Some years ago, a family assembled around the bedside in the last hour of their loved one's life. One said, "I don't know if I believe in heaven."

How are we to think about heaven?

Heaven is both near and different, both utterly close at hand yet completely different from anything in hand. "The kingdom of heaven has come near."[18] "The kingdom of God is at hand for you."[19] "You are not far from the kingdom of God."[20] "The Lord is near."[21] And yet, close as we may be, nothing in our hands is like that which God hands to us.

One way to think about something is to think about its opposites. Our Bible uses the word "heaven" in opposition to the word "earth." Heaven is up there; earth is down here. "As the heavens are high above the earth."[22] "Heaven and earth will pass away, but my words will not pass away."[23] "Let heaven and earth praise

---

17. 1 John 4:7-12, NRSV.
18. Matthew 3:2; Matthew 4:17, NRSV.
19. Luke 10:9a, NRSV.
20. Mark 12:34, NRSV.
21. Phil 4:5, NRSV.
22. Ps 103:11, NRSV.
23. Matt 24:35; Mark 13:31; Luke 21:33, NRSV.

him, the seas and everything that moves in them."[24] In the Bible, as for the ancient philosophers, heaven represents the ultimate or penultimate reality of the physical world. But today we are reluctant to think about heaven as "up there," for astronomy has shown us the physical "up there" that comprises the moon, the Milky Way, and the expanding, even infinite, universe.

Our Bible also speaks of heaven in contrast to hell. The comparison, mind you, is not directional, not between up and down but rather between lasting good and lasting bad. Heaven is good; hell is bad. But we have some questions about these inherited, mythological accounts of hell, as we do about similarly styled accounts of heaven. Harps, wings, clouds . . . fire, forks, tails. Good we acknowledge; evil we acknowledge. Hell as the absence of God, or as the absence of good, we acknowledge. But hell as eternal torment, administered in punitive ways by a divinity of somewhat unpleasant temperament? This hell, we question.

Here is a third contrast: not heaven and earth, not heaven and hell, but heaven and hurt. "Hell is truth seen too late," wrote W.S. Coffin.[25] This contrast is built on time, rather than on space or on morals. Not up and down, not good and bad, but now and then. Heaven is then, earth is now. A belief in heaven, then, is a trust in "what is taking place" over against a knowledge of "what is in place." What is taking place, contrasted with what is in place. What is at hand, as contrasted to what is in hand.[26] "For now we see in a mirror, dimly, but then we will see face to face."[27]

1 Corinthians 15 prepares us, in the form of the Apostle Paul's treatise on resurrection, for the lifelong work of response to the question of heaven. At the heart of Corinthians, and in the marrow of all Easter gospel, is the truth that "something happened." Whatever happened—though its telling may differ according to the

---

24. Ps 69:34, NRSV.

25. Coffin, *Credo*, 53.

26. I am indebted here to the work of my teacher, Dr. Christopher Morse, especially his book *Not Every Spirit: A Dogmatics of Christian Disbelief.* New York: Continuum, 1994.

27. 1 Cor 13:12, NRSV.

teller—was an actual experience in life. Paul tells about resurrection largely on the basis of experience. And while heaven and resurrection are not equivalent terms, they do go together in the basic sense that they both propose freedom from death. The resurrection is Christ's *victory over death, when no other victory avails.*

Paul wrote 1 Corinthians around AD 53–54. This text addresses the following questions in the life of a congregation both contentious and licentious, during a time of transition.

- What kind of person should lead the church through transition, and how shall the church be led?
- What is true wisdom?
- What do we mean by "spirituality"?
- In what may we take pride?
- How do we determine our treatment of people who mistreat others, and so discipline misbehavior? What use to us is the court of law?
- Is marriage a bane or blessing, sinful or soulful?
- May one eat food sacrificed to idols, and otherwise participate in secular culture?
- What is the extent of freedom?
- How much disorder is good in worship?
- What is the relationship between women and men in the church?

Last, Paul writes to address an argument in the church about resurrection. This in itself is utterly fascinating, as it demonstrates that church disagreement about resurrection existed thirty years after Jesus' crucifixion!

Paul sits at the bedside, in earshot of the question of knowing and believing, of heaven and resurrection. He takes your hand and remembers your experience in receiving an inherited tradition: dead, buried, and raised on the third day. With his hand on your shoulder, Paul describes to you the centrality of resurrection to the whole of Christian preaching. He pauses to place this account of resurrection into an apocalyptic frame, which he probably brought with him from Judaism, but notices your flagging interest in the history of religions and so—as he did with circumcision in Galatians, and as we are perhaps inclined to think he often did in polemic—Paul lets the whole Gospel ride on this one point, at this point.

He asks for your experience. (What is your actual experience of life, death, love, the numinous?). He recites names of people to whom the risen Christ appeared, people you also have heard of—Peter, James, apostles, others—and recounts their experiences in addition to his, Paul's own, which serves as our one and only primary source to a personal experience of the risen Christ. He points to popular religious practices, such as the convention, apparently known in the Corinthian church, of baptizing in the name of the dead.

A lengthy pause. Then Paul shares his own dramatic experience of suffering and risks of death, as sure evidence of the power of resurrection. He pointedly equates denial of resurrection with license to do as we please. Paul even takes up, less intelligibly and more mystically, the further question of how resurrection happens. He then philosophizes, and lengthily, about our experiences of the glories of nature, the created order, the firmament, the physical body. The passage is based on experience. While Paul starts with his own experience, he leans heavily on yours.

Then his conclusion. Listen, too, for what is *not* said. For all the experiential assurance of the chapter, Paul clearly announces that he tells of a . . . mystery. Not a fact. A mystery. Not a miracle. A mystery. Not a wonder. A mystery. Not evidence or verdict. A mystery . . . "Listen, I will tell you a mystery!"[28]

To announce this mystery, the New Testament conveys three different accounts of resurrection, including Paul's account in 1 Corinthians 15. Peter, representing the first three Gospels, emphasizes a *physical resurrection*—an empty tomb more than resuscitation, to be sure, but physical nonetheless. Paul emphasizes a

28. 1 Cor 15:51, NRSV.

spiritual resurrection, known through revelation. John announces an *existential resurrection:* one that fills all of life and creation, that was presaged by the raising of Lazarus, that makes the cross itself a glorification, a completion. Peter shows us an *empty tomb;* Paul blows the *trumpet of heaven;* John acclaims a *full heart.* Three accounts to affirm that something happened. Three emphases to reach, whether by mission or providence, together and separately, each of the varied hearts and minds of their hearers, all the spots on the personality map. Something for dreamers, doubters, and doers. Something for engineers, philosophers, and politicians. You may ask if the accounts are all in agreement. In good Methodist fashion, we reply, "They are singing out of the same hymnal." Sings Peter, "Ours the cross, the grave, the skies";[29] sings Paul, "My chains fell off, my heart was free";[30] sings John, "He walks with me and he talks with me."[31]

What the church has tried to name, over the centuries, on Easter, is that something happened. Something physical, something spiritual, something experiential. There is room, here, for your particular temperament. To some measure, they must all be true. For the physical resurrection—the resurrection of the body—is attested, at the least, in the ongoing life of the church. *The church is alive.* And the spiritual resurrection is attested, at least, in the preaching of the faith. *The future is open.* And the existential resurrection is attested, at least, in unexpected, undeserved, real love. *Love is real.*

V. Appendix: Resurrection Voices

With the intention, always, to walk in the gospel in partnership, here our exercise expands to consider the perspectives of other preachers, scholars, and lay leaders who have written or spoken about themes of resurrection.

---

29. Wesley and Wesley, *Collection of Hymns*, 459.
30. Wesley and Wesley, *Collection of Hymns*, 146.
31. *United Methodist Hymnal*, no. 314.

1. William Sloane Coffin

The Rev. William Sloane Coffin, who had been our pastor at Riverside Church in New York, was a dear mentor whose example, service, and preaching were a beacon and guide for us. He had a gift for epigrams, a capacity to put things simply and say things briefly. These are some of my favorites, from his book *Credo*.

"Rules at best are signposts, never hitching posts."[32]

"The woman most in need of liberation is the woman in every man."[33]

"Clearly the trick in life is to die young as late as possible."[34]

"The longest, most arduous trip in the world is often the journey from the head to the heart."[35]

"It is often said that the Church is a crutch. Of course it's a crutch. What makes you think you don't limp?"[36]

"Good preaching is never *at* people; it's *for* people."[37]

"There is more mercy in God than sin in us."[38]

Through the power of faithful preaching, and the power in preaching faith, Coffin also taught many of us this physical resurrection truth: resurrection comes in preaching. He died just before Easter in 2006. With his burial, his voice and words moved out of the swirling eddies in the river of life and loss, and out onto the higher ground of memory. His words carry at least as well from the other side of the river as they did on this side.

> It was in response to the opposition—so many scholars believe—that the doctrine of the empty tomb arose, not as a cause but as a consequence of the Easter faith. The last chapter of Matthew may be literally true—I don't want to dispute it—but I also don't want any of you to

---

32. Coffin, *Credo*, 22.
33. Coffin, *Credo*, 36.
34. Coffin, *Credo*, 121.
35. Coffin, *Credo*, 126.
36. Coffin, *Credo*, 137.
37. Coffin, *Credo*, 154. (Emphasis in the original.)
38. Coffin, *Credo*, 172.

stumble forever over it. Like many a miracle story in the Bible, it may be an expression of faith rather than a basis of faith.[39]

Of course, life after death can no more be proved than disproved. "For nothing worth proving can be proven, nor yet disproven," as Tennyson said. As a child in a womb cannot conceive of life with air and light—the very stuff of our existence—so it is hard for us to conceive of any other life without the sustaining forces to which we are accustomed. But consider this: If we are essentially spirit, not flesh; if what is substantial is intangible; if we are spirits that have bodies and not the other way around, then it makes sense that just as musicians can abandon their instruments to find others elsewhere, so at death our spirits can leave our bodies and find other forms in which to make new music.[40]

To me, it is hard to believe a loving God would create loving creatures that aspire to be yet more loving, and then finish them off before their aspirations are complete. There must be something more.[41]

Love is not façade but God—an experience of God, and an existential resurrection.

2. Nancy Mikell Carruth

One sweltering afternoon, thirty Methodists squeezed into a meeting room fit for twenty-five. From two o'clock to five, the room was so full of flesh that only reluctantly did one add any spirit or word. As personal space disappeared, so did side conversations. After the three-hour meeting and sauna, though, I was given a religious experience.

If you need evidence of resurrection, consider the unlikely prospect of a religious experience in a church meeting. It is a

---

39. Coffin, *Credo*, 28.
40. Coffin, *Credo*, 170–1.
41. Coffin, *Credo*, 170.

remarkable thing to be given a religious experience at a church meeting. The distinction between what is in place and what is taking place—the resurrection distinction—became, for a moment, perceptible. In place are all the systems and structures of a world that forgets the poor, the vulnerable, and the isolated. Taking place, discernable here and there as heaven's future moves toward us, are foretastes of glory. Not many; not planned; not finished; not overwhelming. Here and there. Now, and then.

As the room emptied, my seat mate and I got acquainted. Her name was Nancy Mikell Carruth, a dear elderly woman from New Orleans, and a longtime lay leader in southern Methodism. She lived her life in New Orleans, which the gracious solemnity of her slow speech would clearly tell you. With grace, she unraveled a long chain of stories about her beloved city and the unspeakable devastation caused by Hurricane Katrina in 2005. She told about the swamped Hotel Pontchartrain; about the eclipse of places of memory; about hearing, a month earlier, her first symphony since the flood, held in the sports arena. About the profound sense of Good Friday loss still holding her region.

I was stunned when, suddenly, her narrative moved a continent away and two decades into the past. She readily began to tell me about the whole miraculous creation of Africa University more than twenty years ago, to which she had given so much. The initial dream. Tom Trotter's dream. The scores of meetings, "some even in rooms more crowded than this." The attempts to raise money, for a new venture, in an aging church. The conflicts. The decisions of The United Methodist Church to build a continent-wide, first-class university in Zimbabwe. Imagine getting ten million people to agree on something . . . The planning. The diplomacy. The gradual excitement. And then a moment in time, when what is taking place—heaven—spills over into what is in place, here and now.

I loved Tom Trotter and thought the world of him, I remember her saying. *I will never forget the day we rode for the first time toward the site of Africa University, after so many years of long-distance work. We came around the bend, and there it was . . . We saw the new buildings, shining in the sun. I was just overcome. I was so emotional. Tom wasn't any better, sitting right next to me just a puddle of tears. Such a moment . . . I will never forget it.*

And I will never forget Nancy. In faith she named *what is taking place* (God's future)—Africa University, in contrast to *what is in place* (our hurt)—Katrina. Her self-forgetfulness, in story and in life. Her joy at the radiant memory of giving, without denying the hurt of loss. Her natural testimony of faith, which placed the radiant memory of a resurrection moment, like a garment on top of a hard experience in the present, as a means to confess . . . as if to say:

"Weeping may linger for the night, but joy comes with the morning."[42]

"In the cross of Christ I glory, towering o'er the wrecks of time."[43]

"Suffering produces endurance, and endurance produces character, and character produces hope, and hope does not disappoint us."[44]

3. A Great Chorus of Voices

Finally, here is what some other voices have written about resurrection in years past.

"Resurrection is . . . the lifting of personal life into a new dimension of light and power," preached George Buttrick, across the river at Harvard University Memorial Church, years ago. Christianity does not promise "retrogression from the vivid personal into the vague and abstract impersonal. . . ."[45]

> Then how and why may we honorably hope in resurrection? The inner evidence is in the structure of our

---

42. Ps 30:5, NRSV.
43. *United Methodist Hymnal*, no. 295.
44. Romans 5:4–5, NRSV.
45. Buttrick, *Sermons*, 189.

personal life; the outer evidence, meeting the inner evidence as light meets the eye, is in Jesus Christ. . . . [46]

But we should be quick to admit that faith in resurrection, Christ's and ours, is still a faith. The beckonings of God are just that—beckonings, not bludgeonings, not batteries of irrefutable "evidence," not the tyranny of unanswerable logic. Always there is freedom for our choosing and response. . . . Easter sermons must not be overpreached, and their "proofs" should never overprove, for God's beckonings are always by hint and gleam, lest we be coerced.[47]

Martin Luther:

> When the heart clings to the Word, feelings and reasoning must fail. Then in the course of time the will also clings to the Word, and with the will everything else, our desire and love, till we surrender ourselves entirely to the Gospel, are renewed and leave the old sin behind. Then there comes *a different light*, different feelings, different seeing, different hearing, acting and speaking, and also a different outflow of good works. . . . When the heart and conscience cling to the Word in faith, they overflow in works, so that, when the heart is holy, all the members become holy, and good works follow naturally.[48]

W. Saunders: "Resurrection is a reflective interpretation of encounters with the Living One which had the power to convince, to generate new community, to establish an authorized leadership, and to commit to mission."[49]

Peter Berger:

> More so than with any other portion of the New Testament accounts, there is no way in which historical scholarship can establish "what really happened" (which, as Leopold von Ranke put it, is the aim of historical scholarship). . . . Faith in the Resurrection is

---

46. Buttrick, *Sermons*, 189.
47. Buttrick, *Sermons*, 191.
48. Luther, "Easter Sunday," 246. (Emphasis mine.)
49. Saunders, "Resurrection," IDBS, 740.

faith in a pivotal shift in the cosmic drama of redemption, not in (let us say) a televisable occurrence in a Judean graveyard. Obviously, the perception of this shift, first by Jesus' mourning followers and ever since by believing Christians, took place *through and around* this occurrence. But the perception is not dependent upon the empirical circumstances of the occurrence.... With a little straining I could put my opinion on this in a formula derived from Lutheran theology: The Lutheran view of the Eucharist is that Christ is present "in, with, and under" the physical elements of bread and wine, but without the empirical nature of these elements being miraculously changed. By analogy, one might say that the cosmic event of the Resurrection took place "in, with, and under" the occurrences in Jerusalem at that time, but the event was not and is not dependent on "what really happened" empirically.[50]

Paul Tillich: "Participation, not historical argument, guarantees the reality of the event upon which Christianity is based."[51]

Charles Rice, with Edmund Steimle: "The biblical preachers, including Jesus, intending to communicate the experience of faith, spoke to their contemporaries in the concrete images of the world at hand. The specific task of communicating the gospel led them at once to the willingness to range through the world and speak of God in terms of that world. There can be no question about the meeting of Christianity and culture in the biblical witness to God's work in Jesus Christ. Edmund Steimle is quite right: 'The sermon which starts in the Bible and stays in the Bible is not Biblical.'"[52]

Laurie Mann-Strenge, a Marsh Chapel community member:[53]

> Dean Hill,
>
> First, let me apologize for not responding to your telephone call—at least what I believe was your call—a

---

50. Berger, *Questions of Faith*, 66–67. (Emphasis in the original.)
51. Tillich, *Systematic Theology Vol. 2*, 114.
52. Rice, *Interpretation and Imagination*, 2.
53. Laurie Mann-Strenge, email message to author, April 9, 2020. Message has been lightly edited for clarity.

week last Monday. Like many these days, my cell phone filled up with messages as I worked to get my co-workers and judges up and running remotely. I found what I believed was your message on Monday this week, and immediately decided, in the flurry, that I would listen to it in prayerful silence so I could better respond. I sat down this morning with my coffee and devotions, determined to find peace of mind to respond to you after listening to your voicemail. And, of course, I discovered I had deleted it in error along with the pile of phone calls from attorneys and staff. I am bitterly disappointed not to hear your message in full.

I am so very sorry and most disappointed. Your sermons and services these past three weeks have articulated the backbone of my faith and affirmed my confidence and fears and grief as we approached, and now walk through, Holy Week. Three weeks ago, you honored the shock and awe of stopping and standing still. The fear and the unknown. Life arrested and frozen in time. The absolute grief of cancelling the Easter lily order. The service closed with "How Can I Keep from Singing," which, more than any other hymn, articulates my personal testimony.

Two weeks ago, you meditated on the concept of fallow ground, as I built a temporary "dorm" room for my displaced Northeastern freshman in the basement for his studies and watched the reminders from the family calendar flip by, every few hours, on my cell phone (Dad on road; Mom work, Court, 8–5; Kat dance, 3–6; Annelore volleyball, 7–9; Mom work, Sun and Ski, 5–9). And you honored St. Teresa, whose prayers inspire me as they start the days for the online students at Notre Dame Academy in Hingham. Oh, the fear that grips historians like me, in days like these. The fear as gun sales surge and dictators rise. You even called out the Mary/Martha paradox that I, as one of deep faith and a deep need to control everything, constantly write about. And I scramble still to order more groceries online.

Finally, last Sunday, you spoke with unfailing clarity about the cross. About Christ the Man of Sorrows. About Isaiah. Decades ago, a new graduate from Eastern

Nazarene College, I listened to my mom screaming in the depths of her addiction and mental illness. The *Messiah* was blasting on the stereo as I frantically vacuumed in an attempt to drown out the noise of her lifetime of illness. I heard at last—blasting through the shouting and the roar of the vacuum, after hearing this music all my life—the declaration and affirmation of Isaiah. "Surely! Surely! Surely, he has born our grief and carried our sorrows." In that moment, I finally understood the cross. That was not a call to an impossible life of perfection, a rule set, a culture. Rather, the cross was the place of ultimate sacrifice because there is pain in this world. Because evil exists. Because people like my mother were damaged beyond repair in this world, and the collateral damage to our family was irrefutable. Because holocausts and pandemics and social injustice are everywhere. That as the Apostle Paul so eloquently says, "All creation groans." The cross was the place to take my pain and isolation. The cross is my place of ultimate healing and hope.

"With his stripes we are healed" has been the mantra of his Grace I have seen exemplified ever since: seen in the healing of the medical professionals who helped me usher my mother through her last years; seen through the grace my father has found in the halls of your chapel and the beautiful friendships he carries there. Seen in the healing that continues to come. Seen in the grace of both ordinary and extraordinary days. His grace reaches us even in hell, when we are beyond hope and faith. As Timothy says, "If we are faithless, he remains faithful, for he cannot deny himself." How powerful is the cross! How powerful is grace! How powerful is hope!

This pandemic reveals the horrible social divide that leaves us, as I have felt for some time but now more than ever, in a social structure more medieval than anyone wants to admit. Cell phones do not replace running water, health care, fair wages, fair courts, fair political systems. The poor are abundant and suffering; the middle class is scant and struggling. The wealth is in the hands of a few with mega churches, wielding political power financed on the backs of their poor and faithful.

Thank you for the ministry to my dad. I have been listening with him every week by sitting outside his window while on the phone, or just on the phone.

Thank you again for your ministry, for your church, for your amazing staff and community. Thank you for speaking so deeply to our hearts each week. Forgive my epistle to you, but I felt the need to share how deeply your message speaks to me personally and my gratitude for your ministry, your witness, your healing presence for so very many in the BU community and beyond. You know my father's gratitude knows no bounds. He hungers for the communion that comes with being with you all.

Blessings to your family on this sacred holiday, and blessings and prayers for your safety. Please take no risks. Thank you, again, for the difference you have made in my father's life and in the life of my family.

Blessings on Easter.

My husband, my children, and I will be gathered in prayer outside my dad's window as we listen and celebrate with the community in prayer.

8

Afterward

To those of you who have come to this gymnasium to exercise, I offer my gratitude. Our afterward here is no postlude, no conclusion, to the unfinished work in liberal biblical theology; rather, one may find here some useful directions toward other forms of practical exercise offered to those seeking further engagement with liberal biblical theology, that they may, so to speak, add their own chapters to this ongoing and significant work.

The website of the Boston University Marsh Chapel (www.bu.edu/chapel), under the Dean's page, offers a connection to another book-length work—and workout—with historical, exegetical, theological, and academic perspectives. Five discreet exercises are there available: Hebraic, Johannine, patristic, theological, and historical. In composite, these five are a length similar to the book you have just finished.

- The *Hebraic* exercise celebrates and honors the matchless, eloquent work of Samuel Terrien.
- The *Johannine* exercise works us through the stellar interpretative work of C.H. Dodd, in concert and comparison with other related scholarship.

AFTERWARD

- The *patristic* exercise brings the life work of Cyril Richardson, as an overview of what the early Christian writers—the first generations of post-biblical interpreters, the first biblical and liberal theologians—constructed. Of all current lacunae in theological and pastoral reflection, this is surely one of the greatest.

- The *theological* exercise again shifts the angle of vision, this time to a sort of "proof in the pudding" portion, an overview of five favorite liberal biblical theologians: Terrien, Collins, Sanders, Dunn, and Walton, scholars with whom I have had some personal connection as well as philosophical congruence. Terrien I knew at Union Theological Seminary; Sanders I knew at Union, at Colgate Rochester Crozer Divinity School, and at Claremont School of Theology; and Walton I knew here in Boston, at Harvard Memorial.

- The *historical* exercise marches us, say, on a seaside day hike through some of the most recent AAR/SBL[1] rehearsals of biblical theology—a selective collection to be sure, but representative enough for the last decade or so (Dunn, Brueggemann, and Morgan; and, as a younger representative, a doctoral student, Donahue-Martens). It should be noted that on the whole, though fine essays, these nonetheless fall quite short of what an earlier generation produced (Stendahl, Barr, Childs, others).

A wealth of offerings will engage the reader on various angles of liberal biblical theology, whether in exercise or other form. One may find, on the Marsh Chapel Sermon Archive (blogs.bu.edu/sermons), other works by this author, including the texts of weekly sermons from 1999 to the present, which are searchable according to particular passages, themes, and seasons (both cultural and liturgical).

Among the many titles that offer perspectives from each and various sides of Wesley's quadrilateral, here follows a foursome that may be appreciated by one who, say, teaches a Sunday school class

---

1. American Academy of Religion/Society of Biblical Literature.

in Nebraska, or convenes a Lenten study in suburban Washington, D.C., or serves as chaplain of a small private school in New England, or gathers a book club in downtown San Francisco.

Throckmorton Jr.'s *Gospel Parallels*, to discuss biblical narrative.

Gary Wills' *Head and Heart: American Christianities*, for some perspective on the way traditions change.

Francis Collins' *The Language of God*. He can teach us to reason together.

Andrew Bacevich's corpus of articles and books, which—by reflecting what his hero, Reinhold Niebuhr, called the "spiritual discipline against resentment"[2] needed to avoid an endless cycle of retribution—may help us remember the value of experience.

---

2. Niebuhr, *Moral Man*, 248.

Bibliography

Archbold, Rich. "Obituary—Pastor fought for equal rights." *Long Beach Press-Telegram (CA)*, October 30, 2018: 1. https://www.presstelegram.com/2018/10/29/obituary-the-rev-ken-mcmillan-gave-a-voice-to-voiceless.

Ashton, John. *The Gospel of John and Christian Origins*. Minneapolis: Fortress, 2014.

Berger, Peter L. *Questions of Faith: A Skeptical Affirmation of Christianity*. Oxford, UK: Blackwell, 2004.

Bonhoeffer, Dietrich. *Ethics*. Edited by Clifford J. Green. Translated by Reinhard Krauss, Charles C. West, and Douglas W. Stott. Vol. 6 of *Dietrich Bonhoeffer Works*. Minneapolis: Augsburg Fortress, 2005.

———. *Letters and Papers from Prison*. Edited by John W. de Gruchy. Translated by Isabel Best, Lisa E. Dahill, Reinhard Krauss, and Nancy Lukens. Vol. 8 of *Dietrich Bonhoeffer Works*. Minneapolis: Augsberg Fortress, 2009.

———. *London: 1933–1935*. Edited by Keith W. Clements. Translated by Isabel Best. Vol. 13 of *Dietrich Bonhoeffer Works*. Minneapolis: Augsburg Fortress, 2007.

Brown, Raymond E. *The Community of the Beloved Disciple*. New York: Paulist, 1979.

Brueggemann, Walter, "Suffering Produces Hope." Dr. A. Vanlier Hunter Jr. Memorial Lecture, sponsored by the Institute for Christian and Jewish Studies, Baltimore, MD, April 2, 1998. jcrelations.tripod.com/hope.html.

Bultmann, Rudolf. *Faith and Understanding*. 1st U.S. ed. New York: Harper & Row, 1969.

———. *The History of the Synoptic Tradition*. United Kingdom: Harper & Row, 1963.

Buttrick, George Arthur. *Sermons Preached in a University Church*. Nashville: Abingdon, 1959.

BIBLIOGRAPHY

Caird, G. B. *The New Testament View of Life (Inaugural Lecture)*. Montreal: McGill University Press, 1951.

Coffin, William Sloane. *Credo*. Louisville: Westminster John Knox, 2006.

Cole, David. "Originalism's Charade." *New York Review of Books*, November 24, 2022.

Collins, Francis. *The Language of God: A Scientist Presents Evidence for Belief*. New York: Free Press, 2006.

Collins, John J. *Encounters with Biblical Theology*. Minneapolis: Augsburg Fortress, 2005.

Curry, Michael B., and Sara Grace. *Love is the Way: Holding on to Hope in Troubling Times*. New York: Avery, 2020.

Dickinson, Emily. "This World is not Conclusion." 1896. In *The Poems of Emily Dickinson: Reading Edition*, edited by Ralph W. Franklin, 171. Cambridge, MA: Belknap, Harvard University Press, 1999.

Dodd, Charles Harold. *The Interpretation of the Fourth Gospel*. 1953. Reprint, Cambridge: Cambridge University Press, 1965.

Edwards, Jonathan. "Heaven Is a World of Love (Charity and Its Fruits, Sermon Fifteen, 1738)." In *The Sermons of Jonathan Edwards: A Reader*, edited by Wilson H. Kimnach, Kenneth P. Minkema, and Douglas A. Sweeney, 242–72. New Haven: Yale University Press, 1999. http://www.jstor.org/stable/j.ctt1nq8z8.19.

Encyclopedia Britannica Online, Academic ed., s.vv. "Cambrian explosion," "dinosaur," "earth," "George Herbert," "Henry Vaughan," "Homo sapiens," "Ordovician Period," "plant," "Q," "T.S. Eliot," accessed August–December 2023, https://academic-eb-com.ezproxy.bu.edu/levels/collegiate.

Eusebius. "Book Six." In *History of the Church*, translated by Philip R. Amidon, 233–81. The Fathers of the Church: A New Translation. Washington, D.C.: Catholic University of America Press, 2016.

Fromm, Erich. *Escape from Freedom*. New York: Rinehart, 1941.

Frost, Robert. *The Poetry of Robert Frost*. Edited by Edward Connery Lathem. First Owl Books ed. New York: Henry Holt, 1979.

Harper, Ralph. *On Presence: Variations and Reflections*. Philadelphia: Trinity International, 1991.

Havel, Vaclev. *Disturbing the Peace: A Conversation with Karel Hvizdala*. 1st American ed. New York: Knopf, 1990.

Herbert, George. *The Temple: Sacred Poems and Private Ejaculations*. United Kingdom: G. Bell, 1904.

Hill, Robert Allan. "An Exercise in Liberal Biblical Theology: McGill University Lecture and Symposium, October 21, 2022." *Journal of the Council for Research on Religion (JCREOR)* 4, no. 2 (August 2023): 81–94. https://creor-ejournal.library.mcgill.ca

———. "'No Male and Female': Ruminations on the New Creation." In *Missio Dei and the United States: Toward a Faithful United Methodist Witness*, 103–19. Nashville: General Board of Higher Education and Ministry, The United Methodist Church, 2018.

BIBLIOGRAPHY

James, William. *The Varieties of Religious Experience: A Study in Human Nature.* New York: Longmans, Green, 1902.

Job, Rueben P., and Neil M. Alexander, eds. *Finding Our Way: Love and Law in The United Methodist Church.* Nashville: Abingdon, 2014.

Johnson, James Weldon. "The Creation." In *God's Trombones: Seven Negro Sermons in Verse,* 17–20. New York: Viking, 1927.

Karmanau, Yuras, Adam Schreck, and Cara Anna. "More than 10,000 killed in Mariupol." *Toronto Star,* April 12, 2022. Factiva.

Kendi, Ibram X. *How to Be an Antiracist.* New York: One World, 2019.

King, Martin Luther, Jr. *Letter from Birmingham City Jail.* Philadelphia: American Friends Service Committee, 1963.

Lawrence, Brother, and Joseph de Beaufort. *Brother Lawrence: The Practice of the Presence of God the Best Rule of a Holy Life, Being Conversations and Letters of Nicholas Herman of Lorraine (Brother Lawrence).* New York: Fleming H. Revell, 1895. Google Books.

Lincoln, Abraham. "Speech to One Hundred Fortieth Indiana Regiment." In *Volume 8,* 360–2. Vol. 8 of *The Collected Works of Abraham Lincoln,* edited by Roy P. Basler. New Bruswick, NJ: Rutgers University Press, 1953–1955.

Long, Thomas G. "Chronicle of a Death We Can't Accept." *New York Times,* November 1, 2009. ProQuest Historical Newspapers.

Lowell, James Russell. "The Present Crisis." In *Poems of James Russell Lowell,* edited by Nathan Haskell Dole, 199–203. New York: Thomas Y. Crowell, 1898. Google Books.

Luther, Martin. "Easter Sunday. Second Sermon. Mark 16:1-8." In *Sermons on Gospel Texts for Epiphany, Lent, and Easter,* 238–47. Vol. 2 of *Sermons of Martin Luther,* translated and edited by John Nicholas Lenker. Grand Rapids, MI: Baker, 1988. Reproduction of *The Precious and Sacred Writings of Martin Luther,* Vol. 11. Minneapolis: Lutherans in All Lands, 1906. Page numbers refer to the 1988 edition.

———. *Lectures on Galatians Chapters 1-4.* Translated and edited by Jaroslav Pelikan. Vol. 26 of *Luther's Works.* Saint Louis: Concordia, 1963.

MacLeish, Archibald. " 'J. B.': A Play in Verse." Boston: Houghton Mifflin, 1986. Internet Archive.

Marcus, Joel. *Mark 1-8: A New Translation with Introduction and Commentary.* Vol. 27 of *The Anchor Yale Bible,* edited by William Foxwell Albright and David Noel Freedman. New Haven: Yale University Press, 2005. First published 2000 by Doubleday (New York).

———. *Mark 8-16: A New Translation with Introduction and Commentary.* Vol. 27A of *The Anchor Yale Bible,* edited by John J. Collins. New Haven: Yale University Press, 2009.

Martyn, J. Louis. *Galatians: A New Translation with Introduction and Commentary.* Vol. 33A of *The Anchor Bible,* edited by William Foxwell Albright and David Noel Freedman. New York: Doubleday, 1997.

Morse, Christopher. *Not Every Spirit: A Dogmatics of Christian Disbelief,* 2nd ed. United Kingdom: Bloomsbury Academic, 2009.

BIBLIOGRAPHY

New York Times. "An Immortal Poem," July 6, 1923. ProQuest Historical Newspapers.

Niebuhr, Reinhold. *Moral Man and Immoral Society: A Study in Ethics and Politics*. New York: Charles Scribner's Sons, 1932. 2nd ed. reprinted with forward by Cornel West. Louisville: Westminster John Knox, 2013.

Perrin, Norman. "Son of man." In *The Interpreter's Dictionary of the Bible, Supplementary Volume*, edited by Keith Crim, Lloyd Richard Bailey Sr., Victor Paul Furnish, and Emory Stevens Bucke, 833–6. Nashville: Abingdon, 1976.

Pope, Alexander. *An Essay on Criticism*. 7th ed. London, 1728. Eighteenth Century Collections Online.

Rice, Charles L. *Interpretation and Imagination: The Preacher and Contemporary Literature*. Philadelphia: Fortress, 1970.

Runyon, Theodore. *The New Creation: John Wesley's Theology Today*. Nashville: Abingdon, 1998.

Sanders, James A. "Adaptable for Life: The Nature and Function of Canon." In *Magnalia Dei, the Mighty Acts of God: Essays on the Bible and Archaeology in Memory of G. Ernest Wright*, edited by Frank Moore Cross, Werner E. Lemke, and Patrick D. Miller Jr., 531–60. Garden City, NY: Doubleday, 1976.

Saunders, Ernest W. "Resurrection in the NT." In *The Interpreter's Dictionary of the Bible, Supplementary Volume*, edited by Keith Crim, Lloyd Richard Bailey Sr., Victor Paul Furnish, and Emory Stevens Bucke, 739–41. Nashville: Abingdon, 1976.

Schaller, Lyle. *44 Questions for Congregational Self-Appraisal*. Nashville: Abingdon, 1998.

———. *Strategies for Change*. Nashville: Abingdon, 1993.

Shakespeare, William. *The Complete Works of William Shakespeare*. Edited by G. C. Clark and W. A. Wright. United Kingdom: Parragon, 2000.

Smart, James D. *The Strange Silence of the Bible in the Church: A Study in Hermeneutics*. Philadelphia: Westminster, 1970.

Society of Biblical Literature. *The SBL Handbook of Style*. Atlanta: Society of Biblical Literature, 2014.

Strauss, David A. "Common Law Constitutional Interpretation," *The University of Chicago Law Review*, Vol. 63, No. 3 (Summer 1996): 877.

Swift, Art. "In U.S., Belief in Creationist View of Humans at New Low." *Gallup*, May 22, 2017, https://news.gallup.com/poll/210956/belief-creationist-view-humans-new-low.aspx.

Terrien, Samuel. *The Elusive Presence: The Heart of Biblical Theology*. San Francisco: Harper & Row, 1978.

The United Methodist Church. *The Book of Discipline of The United Methodist Church*. Nashville: United Methodist Publishing House, 2008.

Thurman, Howard. *Jesus and the Disinherited*. Boston: Beacon, 1996.

———. *With Head and Heart: The Autobiography of Howard Thurman*. Orlando: Harcourt Brace, 1979.

BIBLIOGRAPHY

Tillich, Paul. *Existence and The Christ.* Vol. 2 of *Systematic Theology.* Chicago: University of Chicago Press, 1957.

———. *Life and the Spirit, History and the Kingdom of God.* Vol.3 of *Systematic Theology.* Chicago: University of Chicago Press, 1963.

Tittle, Ernest Fremont. *The Foolishness of Preaching and Other Sermons.* New York: Henry Holt, 1930.

———. *Jesus After Nineteen Centuries.* New York: Abingdon, 1932.

The United Methodist Hymnal: Book of United Methodist Worship. Nashville: United Methodist Publishing House, 1989.

Vaughan, Henry. "The Night." In *Silex Scintillans: Sacred Poems and Private Ejaculations. the Second Edition, in Two Books; by Henry Vaughan,* 55–56. London, 1655. ProQuest.

Weeden, Theodore J., Sr. *Mark—Traditions in Conflict.* Philadelphia: Fortress, 1971.

Wesley, John. *Wesley's Standard Sermons: Consisting of Forty-Four Discourses, Published in Four Volumes,* [. . .]. Edited by Edward H. Sugden. 6th annotated ed. London: Epworth, 1966.

———. *The Character of a Methodist[.]* 2nd ed. Bristol, 1742. Eighteenth Century Collections Online.

Wesley, John, George Eayrs, and Augustine Birrell. *Letters of John Wesley.* London: Hodder & Stoughton, 1915. Google Books.

Wesley, John, and Charles Wesley. 1874. *A Collection of hymns for the use of the people called Methodists.* Microform of the original. Toronto: Wesleyan Book Room, 2010. Internet Archive.

www.ingramcontent.com/pod-product-compliance
Lightning Source LLC
Chambersburg PA
CBHW070911160426
43193CB00011B/1426